AMESBURY
History and Descr
South Wiltshire to

by

John Chandler
and
Peter Goodhugh

Second Edition

The Amesbury Society

1989

Published by The Amesbury Society
34 Countess Road, Amesbury, Salisbury, Wiltshire SP4 7AS

First published 1979; Second Edition 1989
© John Howard Chandler and Peter Stephen Goodhugh, 1979, 1989.

All rights reserved. No part of this publication may be reproduced, stored in a retrieval system, or transmitted, in any form or by any means, electronic, mechanical, photocopying, recording or otherwise, without the prior permission of the authors.

The maps in this publication are reproduced with the permission of the Ordnance Survey.

The text of this book is set in 9½pt Plantin Light with headlines in 11pt Plantin Light Italic.

Printed and bound by Salisbury Printing Co. Ltd.,
Greencroft Street, Salisbury, Wilts. SP1 1JF

ISBN 0 9506643 2 4

CONTENTS

FOREWORD TO THE SECOND EDITION

FOREWORD TO THE FIRST EDITION

PART ONE. AMESBURY: A HISTORY by *John Chandler*

CHAPTER ONE: EARLY AMESBURY (to 979)   1
Introduction; The First Inhabitants; Vespasian's Camp; Saxon Amesbury before the Abbey

CHAPTER TWO: THE FIRST ABBEY (979 - 1177)   8
The Foundation of the Abbey; Domesday Amesbury; The End of the First Abbey

CHAPTER THREE: MEDIEVAL AMESBURY   13
The Priory; Pilgrims and Legends; The Medieval Town; The Dissolution

CHAPTER FOUR: LANDLORD, TENANT, AND LAND   25
The Squire; The Tenants; Agriculture

CHAPTER FIVE: THE TRADING TOWN (1539 - 1914)   35
The Clay Pipe Industry; Turnpikes and Stagecoaches; Shopkeepers and Tradesmen

CHAPTER SIX: SOCIAL CHANGE (1539 - 1914)   41
Poverty; Fires; Education; Into the Twentieth Century

PART TWO. AMESBURY: A TWENTIETH CENTURY SURVEY
by Peter Goodhugh

CHAPTER SEVEN: INTRODUCTION 51

CHAPTER EIGHT: THE APPROACHES TO THE TOWN 57
South *(South Mill Hill, The Workhouse, South Mill, Amesbury Electric Light Company, Salisbury Road, Earls Court Road and Parsonage Lane)*; North *(Countess Road)*; East *(The Railway, Boscombe Down, Holders Road, The Drove and Coldharbour, The London Road)*; West *(Stonehenge Road, West Amesbury)*

CHAPTER NINE: AMESBURY PARISH CHURCH 90
Introduction; The Exterior *(The South Transept, The South Aisle, The Nave, The North Transept, The Chancel)*; The Interior *(The South Transept, The South Aisle, The Nave, The North Transept, The Chancel, The Tower, The Saxon Cross, Bosses and Corbels)*; Conclusion

CHAPTER TEN: THE CENTRAL AREA 106
Recreation; Church Street; Manorial Life; High Street; The Centre; Smithfield Street; Flower Lane; Salisbury Street; In Conclusion

NOTES 154

BIBLIOGRAPHY 156

INDEX 160

*This book is dedicated
to the memory of*

WILLIAM KEMM
JOB EDWARDS
LEONARD BUCKLAND

Historians of an earlier Amesbury

FOREWORD TO THE SECOND EDITION

When first published this book was intended solely to complement Amesbury's millennium celebrations in 1979, and no long term prospects were seriously considered. However it soon went out of print, and the modest but increasing number of requests over the last ten years for "the Amesbury book", as it has come to be known, have persuaded the Amesbury Society to publish a new edition.

For this second edition the opportunity has been taken to bring the book up to date as far as possible, to reflect new archaeological and historical evidence and interpretations that have appeared since 1979, and to incorporate changes to the town that have occurred, or are currently proposed. The new edition comes at a time when Amesbury is facing major redevelopments, and we hope that by reissuing this book we shall ensure that, in facing an uncertain future, Amesbury's history and character will not be overlooked.

Although parts of this book have been substantially rewritten, we have tried to keep its size and cost within reasonable limits, and so it has not always been possible to describe recent changes in great detail. We hope, nevertheless, that sufficient information is given to record such changes in principle.

We have been particularly helped by the encouragement received from local people and the helpful responses from everyone we asked for assistance. It is sad to record that some of the older people who helped with background information for the first edition are no longer with us. It is also noticeable that, because families have moved and older members have died, some of the source material used earlier is no longer available. If any reader has written or pictorial evidence about Amesbury's history it would be greatly appreciated if they would allow the authors to record it for future reference.

As with the first edition, we would not have been able to produce this book without the help of the many people who have enthusiastically contributed verbal, documentary and pictorial material and who have helped with the arduous task of proof reading and correcting. In particular the following: Andrew Baker, Alison Borthwick, Peter Brown, Margaret Crook, Philip Dover, Carol Exten-Wright, Rob Forrester-Addie, Richard Fraser, Christine Goodhugh, Terry Heffernan, Jim Hopkinson, Mr and Mrs Kenneth Jarman, Barry Keel, Jesse Lawrence, Rodney Pain, Norman Parker, Julian Richards, Mr and Mrs Harold Simmance, Ted Smith, Michael Snook, Anthony Tuff, Austin Underwood, Ray Ware, Alex Wright, and the staffs of Salisbury and South Wiltshire Museum, University of Southampton Library, Wiltshire Archaeological and Natural History Society, Wiltshire County Council, Library and Museum Service, Wiltshire Record Office. Special thanks are extended to Keith Roberts for his cover design, and to Stephen Tilley and his team at Salisbury Printing, for their help and patience.

J.H.C.
P.S.G.

August 1989

FOREWORD TO THE FIRST EDITION

This book has grown out of a suggestion made some two years ago that, as one of the many ways in which Amesbury might celebrate its abbey's millennium, a souvenir history should be produced. The result is perhaps on a more ambitious scale than was originally intended and the attentive reader may sometimes perceive the haste in which it has been written. Nevertheless we hope that it will prove of interest to both residents and visitors, whose appetites for Amesbury's past will have been whetted by the extensive programme of celebrations in the town during 1979.

As suggested by its title, this book falls into two distinct sections, a history and a description. The first six chapters, which form a short history of Amesbury before living memory, are the work of John Chandler. Peter Goodhugh has written a description of the town with illustrations from his collection of early photographs and postcards. This arrangement has led to some duplication and doubtless many omissions, but was nevertheless felt to be more useful to sightseer and student than a more integrated approach. Each author has benefited from the criticisms of the other, but each remains solely responsible for his own section. The maps have been drawn by Barry Keel, and Jim Hopkinson has helped with the reproduction of the photographs.

This project would not have been possible without the help and kindness of many individuals and organisations. A principal regret is that some of those who gave initial inspiration were unable to see the finished work. Our first acknowledgement must be to the many present and former residents of Amesbury who provided detailed background information and the invaluable photographs, in particular: Olive Lady Antrobus, Sir Philip Antrobus Bt., The Antrobus Trustees, Betty Blake, Don Blakely, the late Ivor Buckland, Gerald Burden, Sam Dimer, Freda Dudek, Marjorie Dunford, Harold Eyres, Ralph Eyres, Olive Holmes, Phylis Hunt, Roselle Jones, Leslie Keel, Doris Lawrence, Jesse Lawrence, Olive Lawrence, Margaret Pethybridge, Frank Piesing, May Revett, Edmund Sandell, Kathleen Sims, Edward Snook, Alfred Southey, Alice Todd, Austin Underwood, Florence Williams, and the firms of Amesbury Motorcycles and T L Fuller & Sons.

In addition, it is our pleasant duty to acknowledge the following debts of gratitude: to the unfailingly courteous staff of the Wiltshire Record Office and Salisbury Diocesan Record Office; to the late (and sadly missed) Richard Sandell, honorary librarian of the Wiltshire Archaeological and Natural History Society; to Peter Saunders and his staff at the Salisbury and South Wiltshire Museum; to members of the staff of Wiltshire Library and Museum Service, especially Edward Boyle, Jane Butterworth, Michael Corfield and Rosemary Green; to the librarians of the Universities of Bristol and Southampton; to the librarian of Dr Williams' Library for allowing access to the Evans manuscript; to Country Life magazine; to the Keeper of Public Records; to the A&AEE Boscombe Down; to Desmond Bonney of the Royal Commission on Historical Monuments (England), Salisbury; to Robert Gates of Press 70; to the Amesbury Parish Council for its generous help towards the cost of publication; to Peter Ball, John Buffrey, Roy Canham, Marjorie

Dunford and Peter Nicholson, who have read and commented upon parts of the work in typescript; to Ann and Christine, our long-suffering wives.

J.H.C.
P.S.G.

Feast of Saint Melor May 1979

AMESBURY: A HISTORY

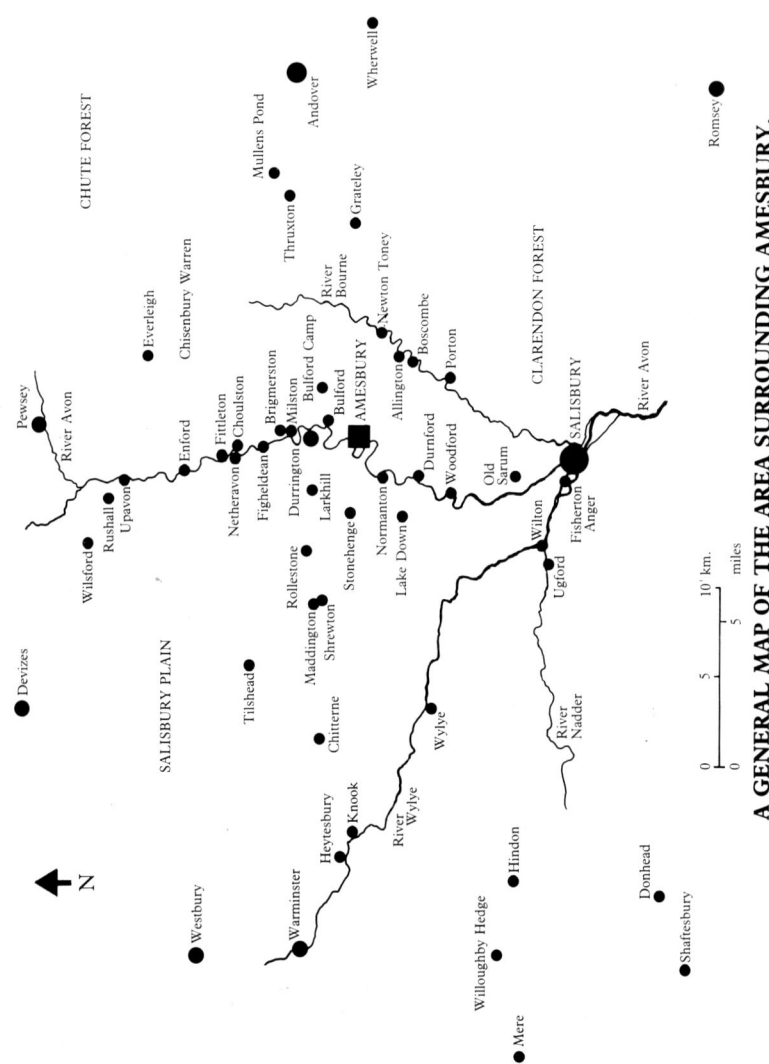

A GENERAL MAP OF THE AREA SURROUNDING AMESBURY, showing places mentioned in the text.

Chapter 1

Early Amesbury (to 979)

Introduction

The subject of this affectionate biography is a small Wiltshire town. Amesbury lies on a meander of the River Avon, eight miles north of Salisbury, at a point where the main road from London to Exeter bridges the river. The chalk downlands of Salisbury Plain surround the town, pocked with remains of earlier civilizations. Until the present century Amesbury depended largely on agriculture, but now its population of some 6,000 inhabitants looks mostly to the neighbouring defence establishments or to Salisbury for their employment. The nucleus of the town and its medieval abbey church remain, although the 'great thoroughfare' which once formed the High Street has been channelled into a modern by-pass. The abbey mansion is now a nursing home, the 18th century houses of the town centre are interspersed with modern shops, and housing estates have encroached onto the common fields. Amesbury may not impress the casual visitor, or even the resident, with a sense of history in the way that Salisbury (an altogether younger place) does, but there is plenty in Amesbury's past that deserves to be remembered.

In fact it would be impossible in a few pages to do justice to more than the thousand years of history which separate the abbey's foundation in 979 from today. Instead this essay examines some of the subjects which seemed to the writer to be the most important in the town's past or the most interesting for the town's present. A great deal remains to be discovered about Amesbury; it is hoped that others will be inspired by this essay to embark on studies of their own.

The First Inhabitants

The foundation of the first abbey was a landmark in the history of Amesbury, but it does not mark the beginning of settlement in the area.[1] The first and most basic of questions, "How old is Amesbury?" cannot be answered by a simple date, and it is by no means easy to know where to begin this history.

Before civilization began the River Avon meandered through the wooded valley beneath the chalk downs, much as today, although the downs themselves were also heavily wooded. To the first nomadic inhabitants of Wessex a river meant water for sustenance but an obstacle to be forded. Casual finds suggest activity in mesolithic and neolithic times to the north of Amesbury, in the vicinity of

Totterdown and Woodhenge, which may reflect an early fording-place, and the Harrow Way, a trackway of venerable antiquity running east-west across southern England, forded the river at Ratfyn, also north of Amesbury. To the earlier neolithic settlers of some 4,000 to 2,500 years before Christ, who set about clearing the forest and cultivating the downs, we owe the long barrows, the great linear earthworks known as the Cursus and the Lesser Cursus, the causewayed enclosure at Robin Hood's Ball near Shrewton and the first building operations at Stonehenge. Such activities must have required a huge workforce and suggest a fairly large and stable population settled in the area. But around 2500 BC a hiatus occurred; Stonehenge seems to have been abandoned for a while, and work was concentrated on sites nearer the river. To this period we owe the henge monuments at Durrington Walls, Woodhenge and Coneybury (the latter excavated in 1980).

The return to Stonehenge, and its embellishment with great sarsen stones from the Marlborough Downs, bluestones from the Preseli mountains of west Wales, and a great ceremonial avenue pointing towards the summer sunrise, may be dated to a few centuries around 2000 BC. This was a time of great technical and artistic innovation in the prehistoric world, when new ideas from the continent swept across Wessex, and produced a bronze age culture of wealth and sophistication which was centred on the area around Stonehenge. Apart from the engineering marvel of Stonehenge itself, which it has been estimated must have taken more than 1½ million man-hours to construct,[2] hundreds of round barrows of various kinds were raised in honour of dead leaders, and their weathered remains litter the Stonehenge landscape. The few square miles of downland which now overlook Amesbury must have enjoyed fame and national importance at this period such as the town of Amesbury has never achieved.

Alongside the prestigious complex of religious and ceremonial monuments, the day-to-day business of farming the downland developed in a more organised way. Few visible traces of these centuries of hard work survive, but archaeologists have discovered in the Stonehenge area, by excavation or aerial photography, evidence of boundary ditches, small enclosed fields and farmsteads of this late bronze age period. Nearly 30 field systems, of various sizes, have been identified on either side of the River Avon between Upavon and Woodford, and some, such as the important 600 hectare site above Figheldean, Brigmerston and Milston, are known to have been in use during the late bronze age. Most such evidence of prehistoric activity and settlement survives on the chalk downland rather than in the valley, where Amesbury and neighbouring villages sit. This may be because the valley was still too densely wooded, or it may be that human exploitation of the valley during the succeeding centuries, coupled with the natural processes of hillwash and alluvial deposits in the valley floor, have succeeded in obliterating all trace of what went on before. To return to our original question, we may only reply that, although the Amesbury area was, in prehistoric terms, densely populated in neolithic and bronze age times, and was indeed for a while the centre of the prehistoric world, there is no evidence that Amesbury itself, as a community of whatever form, had yet begun.

Vespasian's Camp

If we are looking for the first Amesbury we must turn our attention to Vespasian's Camp, the large (15 hectare) iron age hillfort which lies immediately to the west of modern Amesbury on the west bank of the river.[3] In plan it forms an elongated triangle pointing north, with an extension to the south to meet the meandering river. To the naturally steep west and north-east sides of the spur were added a single bank and ditch, and at the northern tip, where the Harrow Way passed close by, an entrance was made. A second entrance probably existed in the south-east corner, near where the modern Stonehenge Road enters the site. Its title is a product of 18th century antiquarianism and a complete misnomer - Vespasian, the Roman emperor, would have been a very unwelcome visitor to this iron age camp. It may even have been refortified to keep him out, as road-widening in 1964 and a small archaeological excavation in 1987 both revealed a second phase in the fort's construction.[4]

Most hillforts were constructed within a few centuries of 500 BC; at first a single bank and ditch were built to fortify a natural stronghold, and later second and third banks were added to some of the more important sites. No rigid division should be drawn between the hillfort builders and the farmers of earlier centuries, although clearly the political climate at the time required the means of defence from attackers, and there was a sufficiently strong tribal authority to organise the enormous corporate labour involved. Meanwhile agriculture continued, and the remains of iron age fields, enclosures and boundaries are visible on air photographs of Earls Farm Down and elsewhere. This activity was probably organised from Vespasian's Camp, which would also have acted as a distribution and marketing centre. During more perilous periods the farmers and their families could have resorted to the hillfort for protection, but in less troubled times they would have lived in farmsteads and hamlets near their fields (such a settlement is known to have existed on South Mill Hill).

By analogy with hillforts which have been thoroughly excavated, it has been calculated that a fort of the size of Vespasian's Camp could have enclosed a population approaching 1,000. A considerable tract of cultivated land would have been necessary to support so many people, and this raises the question of the hillfort's territory and its relationship with neighbouring communities. The absence of hillforts on the plain to the north-west of Vespasian's Camp is notable, and this downland was probably used to graze the shorthorn cattle and small iron age sheep which manured the arable. Ogbury Camp, an enormous hillfort-type enclosure near Great Durnford, was probably a cattlefold and, because of its proximity to Amesbury, may have come under the control of Vespasian's Camp. Next to the south lies Old Sarum, a very important stronghold, and it may be that, by the time of the Roman invasion, this fort had eclipsed Vespasian's Camp (many hillforts had been abandoned by this time) and controlled all this stretch of the Avon valley.

In 43 AD four Roman legions invaded Britain and one, under the future emperor Vespasian, was employed in knocking out native strongholds in Wessex

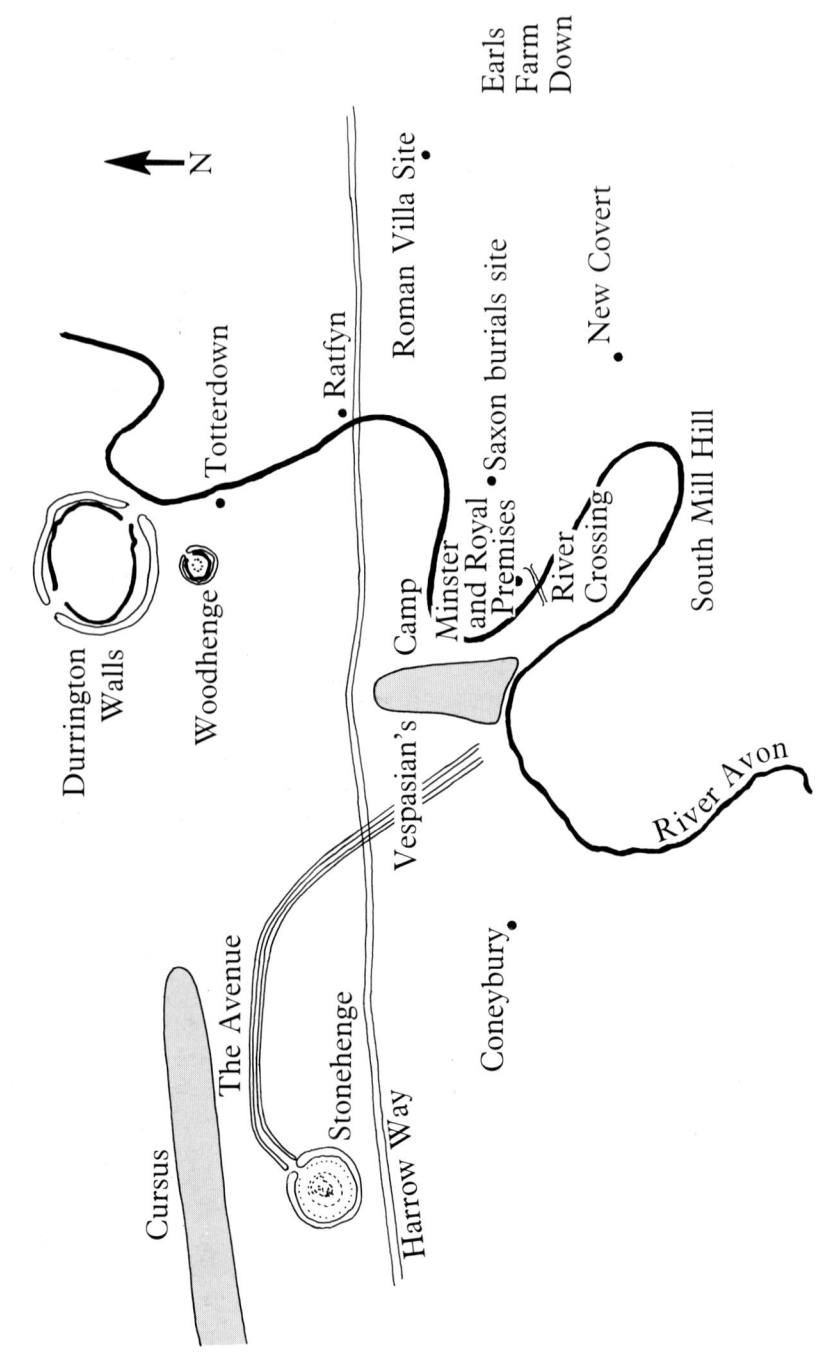

PRINCIPAL ARCHAEOLOGICAL SITES NEAR AMESBURY

and the south-west peninsula. There is no evidence that Vespasian's Camp was one of the twenty hillforts which his biographer claims him as conqueror, but it has been suggested that one line of penetration may have been up the Avon valley and along the Vale of Pewsey towards the Bristol region.[5] Evidence for this is provided by stray finds of Roman weaponry at Wilsford and Bulford, but there is no indication whether Vespasian's Camp played any part in resisting the Roman advance.

Amesbury does not lie in an area colonised by the Romano-British aristocracy living in luxurious villas; indeed the absence of such villas has led to the suggestion that the whole of Salisbury Plain may have been controlled by the Roman government as an imperial estate (not greatly differing from the Ministry of Defence today).[6] But this does not mean that the area was deserted. The land continued to be cultivated by partly Romanised iron age inhabitants living in modest farmsteads, such as may have existed on Earls Farm Down and near Durrington Walls,[7] or in native villages, such as at Chisenbury Warren, Knook and various other sites on Salisbury Plain. Stray finds of Roman material have also been recovered from locations near Amesbury, including Stonehenge, New Covert and indeed from within Vespasian's Camp,[8] although under Roman rule the dangers which had prompted its construction had disappeared, and the hillfort was probably abandoned until such time as it might be needed again.

Saxon Amesbury before the Abbey

A world of shadowy heroes and garbled legends follows the break-up of Roman civilization in Britain in the 5th century, but some scholars, in trying to reconstruct the sequence of events, have speculated that the name "Amesbury" may offer a clue to understanding these obscure times.[9] The earliest documents containing forms of the name - *Ambresbyrig* and *Amberesburg* - although themselves dating from the 11th century and later, refer to transactions several centuries earlier.[10] The second element of the name refers to a *burh* or stronghold, which can hardly be other than Vespasian's Camp, while the first element seems to enshrine the personal name of an owner or ruler. This name may have been something like *Ambri* (Geoffrey of Monmouth thought so when, in telling the legend of Stonehenge, he talked of "the hill of Ambrius"); but could it not instead be referring to the leader of the British resistance against Saxon colonisation, the renowned Ambrosius Aurelianus? If so, the argument runs, then Amesbury might have been the centre of this powerful figure's operations, or at the least a stronghold occupied by warriors - *Ambrosiaci* - loyal to him. If the latter, Amesbury would take its place alongside other sites in the south and south midlands, such as Ambrosden and Amberley, which may also imply by their names that they were outposts of Ambrosian resistance; if the former, then perhaps Amesbury was the headquarters of a large sub-Roman estate controlled by Ambrosius, who is believed to have been a wealthy landowner of the late Roman aristocracy.

This idea, although it will probably never be proved, is not quite as fanciful as it may at first appear, especially if evidence from later periods is considered. In due course in the 6th century the native British resistance, led by Ambrosius, gave way, and much of England was settled and dominated by Saxon and other Germanic tribes. In the Avon valley a Saxon victory at Old Sarum in 552, two generations after Ambrosius, left the way clear for the newcomers to penetrate south Wiltshire. But the so-called Saxon "invasion" is now generally seen to have been a great deal more peaceful and gradual than was formerly believed, and there is an increasing body of evidence to suggest that many boundaries, estates and settlements from Roman and sub-Roman Britain continued relatively unscathed through this transitional period. Now if it can be shown that Amesbury was a place of importance and the centre of an estate during the Saxon centuries it is not impossible that such a role was inherited from an earlier period, when Ambrosius was alive in the 5th century.

The archaeological evidence for Saxon Amesbury before the founding of the first abbey in 979 is as follows: trial excavation at Vespasian's Camp in 1987 failed to find signs of re-occupation in the sub-Roman or Saxon period, but this may have been due to later destruction of evidence by ploughing;[11] however in about 1834 several skeletons of the pagan Saxon period (before about 700) were discovered at the lower end of London Road, near the modern traffic lights, and it is likely that they came from a cemetery in the area, the remainder of which still awaits discovery;[12] one of two Saxon crosses discovered during restoration work on the parish church in 1907 has been tentatively dated on stylistic evidence to the middle or late 10th century, and so may pre-date by a few years the establishment of the abbey;[13] also from the area of the church coins of the reign of Edward the Elder (899-924) discovered during gravedigging in the churchyard have recently been published.[14] These scraps may be coupled with one further place-name, Haradon Hill, an alternative name for Beacon Hill, which is derived from *hearg*, a word used by Saxons to describe a heathen temple, and so was presumably coined when the survival of such a temple was noteworthy, around 700.[15]

Documents tell us that Amesbury belonged to the kings of Wessex from at least the time of Alfred, who died in 899, but probably from much earlier, because the community was taxed not in the usual way, but by an archaic form of levy in kind, sufficient to maintain the king and his retinue for one night. This arrangement had been formalised as early as the 7th century, and Amesbury's status as the centre of a royal estate may therefore stretch back to this period.[16] By the time of the Norman conquest in the 11th century Amesbury was the focal point for a hundred, an administrative area similar in size to the much later rural districts, and this arrangement had probably taken shape unrecorded several centuries earlier. It was credited too with a vast amount of woodland, far more than could have existed within the present parish, even supposing that the chalk downlands were heavily wooded at this period, which is most unlikely. This woodland, it has been suggested, comprised parts or all of the later royal forests of Chute and Clarendon, and so here is another indication that Amesbury's influence extended over a large area of south Wiltshire.[17] Indeed the 11th century estate seems also to have included land at Lyndhurst in Hampshire and Bowcombe on the Isle of Wight.[18]

From all this evidence it is possible to make a few guesses about Amesbury on the eve of the founding of the first abbey in 979. By this date it was already regarded as an old and influential place, by virtue of ancient landholdings in Wiltshire and beyond, and heroic associations stretching back to Ambrosius. But whatever the size or antiquity of its landholdings, the fact that Amesbury was the headquarters of a royal estate meant that it would have acquired premises for the king's staff to administer the land, govern his tenants and collect taxes, as well as for the king himself and his retinue to use as accommodation and for assemblies (which they did in 932 and 995).

Alongside these government premises or royal palace it is very likely that a religious building known as a minster would have existed; it would have acted as the headquarters for priests working throughout the Amesbury estate, and the mother church for all Christian worship in the area.[19] By comparison with other royal estate centres of the period we might also expect the beginnings of a small town to be developing around these headquarters buildings, to serve their needs and to capitalize on the traffic and business that they brought to Amesbury.[20]

Where the palace and minster lay, and in which directions the seeds of the town developed, are matters for conjecture - and perhaps one day for archaeology to solve. However it is not unreasonable to see a river-crossing at or near the present Queensberry Bridge, in the shadow of and guarded by Vespasian's Camp, as a very early element in the town plan, and the position of the present church as the possible site of the Saxon minster, with the royal premises close by, and the town developing along the present High Street.

Such is the picture - necessarily hazy - of Amesbury before its abbey. We might have chosen to embellish it with accounts drawn from the legends of Melor, Guinevere and Merlin; but these legends, so far as they concerned Amesbury, originated towards the end of the medieval period, and it is best that we discuss them in that context.

Chapter 2

The First Abbey (979-1177)

The Foundation of the Abbey

The monastic ideal was not new in the 10th century.[21] Religious communities had existed on the continent since the later Roman empire and were established in Britain by Augustine and his 7th century successors. By the end of the 9th century, however, British monasticism was moribund, and the leaders of the 10th century monastic revival, Aethelstan, Edgar and archbishop Dunstan, adopted completely new sites for many of their foundations. Edgar, whose peaceful reign lasted from 959-975, was a fervent champion of the new monasticism and his views were shared by his second wife, Aelfthryth (Elfrida), who survived him. Edgar's death in 975, before either of his surviving sons had reached manhood, brought about a crisis. The succession passed to Edward, Edgar's son by his first wife, but the sovereignty was contested by supporters of Aethelred, Edgar's son by Aelfthryth. Edward's unpopular reign was turbulent but brief; in 978 he was murdered at Corfe Castle whilst visiting his stepmother, Aelfthryth, and the crown passed to her son, Aethelred, then a boy of about thirteen. Aelfthryth herself can hardly be held responsible for a murder in such embarrassing circumstances; for, whilst she doubtless preferred Edward dead, his blood spilled in her castle gave Aethelred's reign the most inauspicious of beginnings.

The foundation of nunneries at Wherwell[22] near Andover and at Amesbury took place shortly after the assassination, probably therefore in 979. The traditional reason for the foundation, Aelfthryth's penance for the murder of her stepson, can be no more than partly true, especially if as seems likely she was not herself guilty of the treachery. In so far as an act of contrition was necessary, on a political level, in order that the new regime might appear penitent for the heinous crime of its supporters, the tradition is doubtless correct. Edward had not been popular, and did not come to be venerated for a generation, but for the manner of his death his successor required the nation's forgiveness. There was, however, a second reason for the foundations. The death of Edgar and the disputed succession had resulted in rival factions forming among the ruling classes, and, amid the resulting confusion and uncertainty, noblemen hostile to the monastic revival seized the opportunity to recover land that they had lost to the new abbeys.[23] During Edward's short reign some communities may have been dispersed and others lost possessions; monasteries may even have been destroyed. The deliberate foundation of two monastic houses at the beginning of Aethelred's reign may be seen as a reaction to this chaos, a bold assertion by a new regime that it heralded the return of the stability and pro-monastic spirit of Edgar's government.

It is tempting to see the choice of Amesbury as a monastic foundation as in some way connected with the cult of St Melor, to whom, from a very early date, the church has been dedicated. The legend of Melor, which embodies several semi-historical Breton figures, tells of a young prince who was mutilated and later murdered by a wicked uncle to prevent his succession to the throne.[24] When miracles began to occur about his body and severed head his relics were venerated and he took his place in the canon of saints. (Later developments of the legend are discussed below in chapter three.) The relics of Melor probably came to Britain in the first half of the 10th century when many Breton saints were dispersed before invading hordes and their relics found their way to Wessex, whose king, Aethelstan, had close links with Brittany. On the strength of this, and the close correspondence between the careers of Melor and Edward it has sometimes been suggested that a cult of Melor existed at Amesbury before 979, and that it was because of its existence that Aelfthryth chose Amesbury as the site of her new abbey.

This kind of explanation raises more problems than it solves, such as why should the relics of Melor have been at Amesbury in the first place? And in any case such an explanation is not necessary to an understanding of why Amesbury was chosen as the site of a new abbey. Amesbury, as we have seen, was a thriving community at an important river-crossing, in the heartland of old Wessex, which was already noted for famous nunneries (such as Shaftesbury, Wilton, Romsey and Winchester). It was also a royal estate, and so land was readily available within the king's gift to endow the new monastery. But apart from the general suitability of Amesbury without Melor, there is a very grave objection to the Melor theory. At the time of the foundation of Amesbury Abbey Edward had not been venerated; indeed if the foundation preceded the translation of Edward's body to Shaftesbury in 980 the miracles which eventually led to his being styled St Edward, King and Martyr had probably not even begun to be alleged. Even if they had, it was certainly not in Aelfthryth's interest to draw attention to the similarity between Edward and Melor, since she would thereby have glorified her hated stepson and cast herself in the role of Melor's murderous uncle. If, on the other hand, it was Melor who came later to be associated, in the 11th century, with the recently venerated Edward, the otherwise inexplicable connection between Melor and Amesbury is easily explained, and the whole sequence is plausible. Thus it would appear that the relics of Melor came to Amesbury after the foundation rather than preceding it. If this was the case, then their arrival must have occurred before 1031, the latest possible date for a Saxon list of saints' resting-places, which includes a reference to Melor at Amesbury; soon afterwards Amesbury abbey became the main centre of his cult in this country.[25]

Domesday Amesbury

Although we have suggested that the present church may be on the site of the Saxon minster, there is at present no firm evidence of the site of the original abbey buildings. A so-called 'Saxon' column, discovered about 1900 embedded in the eastern end of the nave north wall of the parish church, is now thought to be no earlier than the 12th century, and not, therefore, a part of Aelfthryth's foundation. Indeed, the original monastic church may have been constructed of wood, as at Wilton. However, the reworking of several Norman features in the present church, including the 'Saxon' column, is a clear indication that a building existed on this site before the first abbey was dissolved in 1177. It is therefore possible that the original abbey complex superseded the minster and was on or near the site of the present church.[26]

The presence of a royally-endowed monastery at Amesbury should have provided a stimulus for the development of a town. The arrival of Melor's relics should also have ensured the abbey's success. But although the abbey was doubtless an asset, Amesbury's growth seems to have been checked during the 11th century. The abbey's income remained small, so that it ranked as one of the poorest nunneries in the country. The abbess never attracted any new endowments, nor did she acquire land (and with it influence) in Amesbury itself. Furthermore, Amesbury found that the ancient status which it had enjoyed, by virtue of its royal premises, had largely disappeared once the formerly peripatetic court had become more centralised. It had never in fact been of value to the crown as a revenue-earning estate; and its sole use, as a source of provisions, was now superseded. Many similar royal estates, by the time of the conquest, had been granted burghal status, which conferred on them the right to mint coins, build fortifications and perform a number of trading functions. But not so Amesbury, which thereby stood to suffer from the prosperity of neighbouring *burhs*, such as Tilshead and Bedwyn, royal manors which had formerly been of no greater importance than Amesbury. This failure to develop may probably be attributed to the closeness of Wilton, then a major regional centre, and the ascendancy, encouraged by the government, of Old Sarum in the 11th century.[27]

At the time of the Norman conquest, therefore, Amesbury was something between a village and a town, owned by the king although dominated by a monastery, head of a hundred although not a *burh*. Some idea of life in Amesbury soon after the conquest may be gained from Domesday Book, compiled for William I in 1086. The principal entry for Amesbury begins as follows:

> The king holds Amblesberie. King Edward [the Confessor] held it. It never paid geld, nor was it assessed in hides. There is land for 40 ploughs. In demesne are 16 ploughs and 55 serfs and 2 coliberts. There are 85 villeins and 56 bordars having 23 ploughs. There are 8 mills paying £4.10s and 70 acres of meadow. The pasture is 4 leagues long and 4 leagues broad; woodland 6 leagues long and 4 leagues broad.

Quite apart from its strange terminology Domesday has many pitfalls. As a royal manor Amesbury's possessions were scattered, and it is certain that the totals given, for example of woodland, do not refer exclusively to the community in Amesbury itself. It has been noted also that some figures are approximate, and that even so the units of measurement are flexible. Nonetheless, Domesday is invaluable as a source of information about population and economic activity and as a means of comparison.

The different classes of society are shown clearly by the extract quoted above. Land held directly by the crown (in demesne) was farmed by slaves (serfs) and half-free men (coliberts), and this accounted for nearly half of Amesbury's arable land. The remainder was rented to villagers (villeins) and their social inferiors, cottagers (bordars). The figures for these two groups represent families, not individuals, and so each may represent three, four or more inhabitants. Taking this into account, along with the few tenants of Amesbury lands not held by the crown, and the members of the monastic community, a figure of about 700 may very guardedly be suggested for the total population for the whole estate of Amesbury. On this basis Bedwyn would have been approximately the same size, Tilshead slightly smaller, and two nearby villages on the Avon - Durnford and Netheravon - rather less than half the size of Amesbury.

Land is divided in Domesday into four categories, arable (ploughland), meadow, pasture and woodland. By comparison with other royal manors in Wiltshire Amesbury's quota of arable land was small whilst its woodlands were very large. The number of mills, eight, may seem surprising, and it is much higher than the average for Domesday manors in Wiltshire, but no higher than for some of the other royal manors. The river valleys of south Wiltshire, in fact, boast some of the highest concentrations of watermills anywhere, and Amesbury's eight are not exceptional, although they may well be a further indication that the Domesday estate of Amesbury included places outside the present parish.

The typical Norman community, as depicted in Domesday, was largely self-supporting. Certain commodities, such as salt, had to be obtained from elsewhere, but by and large a village prospered according to the use it made of its land. Amesbury would have been able to earn some additional revenue from trade, since it was situated on, or close to, a main road, was an administrative centre, and lay outside the gates of an abbey. The king's lands were not assessed for the tax known as geld, and so it is hard to see what effect the conquest had on the value of the manor; the single hide in Amesbury owned by Osmund, however, seems to have prospered, since in 1086 it is assessed at double its value in 1065.

The End of the First Abbey

The first abbey was a house of Benedictine nuns. Until the reforming orders of the 12th century and later, which preferred new, isolated sites, most monasteries in England followed the Benedictine rule, and many were established in towns and cities, where they played no mean part in the life of their surroundings.

Surprisingly little is known of the 200 year history (979-1177) of the first abbey, so that any reconstruction must be based to some extent on conjecture.

Whether the original buildings were stonebuilt or wooden is unknown, but they are likely to have consisted of a small, possibly apsidal, church with a cloister surrounded by the conventual buildings. An infirmary perhaps also existed, separated from the other buildings. As we have seen, it is by no means certain that the first abbey succeeded the Saxon minster on the same site, but if we assume that the Norman work in the present church may have belonged to the church of the first abbey, it is clear that rebuilding took place in the early 12th century during the Norman period.[28] This is seen in the nave, where the exterior north wall exhibits blocked Norman clerestory windows above the roof line of a former structure, probably a north aisle. There is no indication now, however, of the length of the 12th century nave or the form of the aisle.

From Domesday we learn that the abbess owned land in several neighbouring villages, Bulford, Boscombe, Allington, Choulston (near Figheldean) and Maddington, as well as a manor in Winterbourne Bassett (north Wiltshire) and lands in Berkshire. The latter may not have been a part of the original endowment but later additions, acquired on the dissolution of an early monastery at Kintbury. Compared with the two other Wiltshire Benedictine houses, Wilton and Malmesbury, Amesbury's income from its estates was small, about one-fifth that of Wilton and one-sixth that of Malmesbury. It seems also to have been vulnerable to encroachment from other landowners, since during the reign of Edward the Confessor two hides in Amesbury had been granted to the abbess of Wilton, and in 1086 the abbey had unjustly lost its holdings at Winterslow. The poverty of the house by comparison with its rivals, and the effect this had on limiting the town's development, should not however lead us to underestimate the importance of the abbey as a source of income and renown to the whole community. Nor should we imagine that the life of the nuns was anything but luxury compared with the squalor of the unfree townspeople outside their gates.

The first abbey ended as it had begun, in an act of political penance for a murder, in this case the murder of Thomas Becket. As penance for his complicity in the crime Henry II was at first required to take part in a crusade, but when this proved impracticable absolution was offered on condition that he founded three religious houses. In the event two - Waltham (Essex) and Amesbury - were refoundations, and only Witham Friary (Somerset) was new.[29] At Amesbury, following an accusation of irregular living by the nuns (possibly well-founded),[30] Henry II appropriated the abbey in 1177 so that he could endow a new foundation and thereby fulfil his vow at the shrine of Becket. Whatever the truth behind the specific charge against the nuns, (and it was never difficult to turn malicious gossip to good advantage), it is certainly true that the Benedictine rule, as observed in the 12th century, appeared to many to be too lax, and hence the movement in favour of new orders, such as that of the nuns of Fontevrault, to whom Amesbury Abbey now passed. In 1177 there were 30 nuns at Amesbury; all appear to have declined an invitation to join their more rigorous successors and were expelled. The abbess, Beatrice, was deposed and pensioned off.

Chapter 3

Medieval Amesbury

The Priory

The decision of the reigning monarch to suppress a mediocre house of nuns and replace it with a lavishly-endowed, splendid new priory of the fashionable Fontevraldine order marks Henry II as one of Amesbury's greatest benefactors.[31] The year 1177, when the decision was taken, is therefore a crucial turning-point in the town's history. In May of that year the king in person saw the first community from the French mother house of Fontevrault installed at the abbey by the archbishop of Canterbury. Ten years later, after grants of land or churches in more than 20 parishes, and very extensive building operations costing the princely sum of £881 to suit the nuns' spiritual and temporal needs, the new priory was complete, and the opening took place on 30th November 1186.

Amesbury was the fourth and last English house of the order of Fontevrault to be established. It was also the largest, and like its mother house in Normandy its

The seal of Isabel de Geneville, elected prioress at Amesbury in 1309. It depicts the prioress kneeling, with the king, seated, above. The building at the top is possibly a representation of Amesbury's monastic church at that time. Reproduced by courtesy of the Society of Antiquaries of London.

nuns were recruited from the ranks of the aristocratic and wealthy.[32] The order differed from all other monastic orders (except Gilbertine) in admitting both male and female religious into one community, although the sexes were segregated by separate conventual buildings, and the women, the prioress in particular, were always the more influential. Double houses, as these communities were called, sprang up in the 12th century and met with mixed success; many, including Amesbury, eventually reverted to single houses.

For the time being Amesbury Priory prospered. Various extensions and improvements to the fabric were made in the early 13th century. Royal patronage continued, and in 1285 two women of the royal family, Mary (Edward I's daughter) and Eleanor of Provence (his mother) entered the community; the king paid repeated visits to Amesbury. By 1317/8 the strength of the priory was 117 nuns and 20 male religious. Ten years later, at a service on Ascension Day, 1327, 36 nuns were consecrated, including the noble Isabel of Lancaster.

There were two flaws, however, in the structure of the priory. The first was a weakness in the Fontevraldine ideal of double houses, which led to tensions between the prioress and her subordinate prior. The second, which it shared with all alien priories, was its vulnerability when England was at war with the country of the mother house, in this case France. Amesbury owed allegiance to Fontevrault, and through Fontevrault to the pope himself. The priory therefore stood outside, in large measure, the control of the English secular and ecclesiastical administration, and was open to reprisals from them in times of war. At Amesbury these manifested themselves in the form of disputes over the succession, the severing of some lines of communication with Fontevrault, and attempts at confiscation.

Crisis point was reached in 1400. A dispute had arisen between the prioress, Sybil Montague (whose appointment and subsequent conduct seem to have been unsatisfactory), and the prior, Robert Dawbeney. After arbitration the matter was not finally resolved, and on 14th March 1400 a group of Dawbeney's supporters, encouraged by some brethren and nuns, imprisoned the prioress and held her hostage for several days inside the convent. Sybil was eventually restored to her position as prioress after a commission of enquiry, but the damage was irreparable. Fontevrault took no part in the dispute, and it appears that the mother house had lost most of its former authority. It is probable that, to all intents and purposes, the priory reverted to a Benedictine house in the 15th century. Nor did the double house arrangement survive this conflict; male religious at Amesbury, of whom there were one priest, seven brethren and one lay brother in 1380/1,[33] disappear after 1400, leaving only the nuns and a chaplain or chaplains to conduct religious services for them, and to act as parish priest for the townspeople.[34]

One problem relating to the priory cannot be ignored, although most of the difficulties have now been overcome. The publication in 1900 of the results of discoveries made during building work at the abbey mansion in 1860 reopened a heated controversy about the precise location of the abbey church and conventual buildings. The issue cannot be finally resolved unless further archaeological investigation takes place, but some attempt may be made at weighing the arguments in the light of knowledge not available in 1900.

The main sources of evidence used in the 1900 arguments were the surviving fabric of the present abbey church, the discovery of tiles, artefacts and the foundations of walls in 1860 on the abbey mansion site, and scattered documentary references. The kingpin of the argument that the present abbey church was the principal priory church rests on a fairly close correspondence (except in the length of the nave) between its measurements and measurements of the priory church taken at the time of the dissolution. It was further argued that the present abbey church is too large not to have been the priory church; also that the predominantly Early English style of the present church is consistent with building work undertaken soon after the refoundation; and that there is architectural evidence of a cloister on the north side of the nave. For such arguments to carry weight it must be conceded that the discoveries on the mansion site, 300 metres north of the church, could not have belonged to the convent proper (which was always grouped around the cloister adjacent to the church) but must have been part of an outlying building, the infirmary complex or the prioress's lodgings.

The principal counter-argument lay in examining the accounts of the dissolution, in which, along with most of the conventual buildings, the priory church was ordered to be destroyed, as being deemed superfluous. It is clear that, by 1542, the priory church was in ruins; and yet in the same year a plumber was paid to repair the chancel roof of the parish church, and a parishioner willed to be buried in the church of St Melore, for which he would provide a number of adornments. Furthermore, the 1860 excavations on the mansion site yielded an object thought to be a holy water stoup (appropriate only to a church), numerous tiles and evidence of molten lead (melting of the lead accompanied the demolition of the church). Indeed the principal room uncovered was conjectured to have been the chapter house, a building which must have been adajcent to the church.

To this list of objections (but a fraction of the many arguments put forward by either side) we would add two observations: firstly, it would have been very odd for the priory church to have been thought superfluous if it were also the sole parish church for a town of significant size; and secondly, if the conventual buildings are drawn out in their usual positions, and in accordance with measurements of lead roofs preserved from the accounts of the dissolution, the convent kitchen would normally have occurred at the north-west corner of the cloister; now we know that the prioress's lodging and associated buildings adjoined the convent kitchen, and further that it was this part of the priory, and this alone, which was retained and subsequently formed the basis of the abbey mansion. If this argument is valid the nave of the priory church must have lain little more than the length of the cloister (about 32 metres) to the south-east of the present abbey mansion. That such a layout existed is substantiated by the observations of William Kemm and his friends, who in June 1870:

> Took a walk in Amesbury park with Mr Job Edwards, Mr J Zillwood and his

son Mr F Zillwood. The season having been a very dry one caused the foundation of the old abbey and of later walls to show, by the grass being parched. The buildings of the ancient abbey were evidently very extensive, reaching 70 or 80 yards from the present house towards the lodge at Grey Bridge [ie. the east]...[35]

This testimony, if the observations are correct, is quite consistent with the normal monastic pattern, and is a strong argument in favour of the 'two churches' theory. The following reconstruction is presented as a hypothesis which seems to fit the known evidence.[36]

In 1177 the incoming prioress and her 21 or 24 accompanying nuns occupied the buildings which already existed, probably adjoining the present parish church on its northern side. By 1186 a new church and conventual buildings had been built to the north of the existing church, near the abbey mansion site, to which the nuns transferred, vacating the original abbey buildings for use by the male religious (who had arrived by 1189). The church which exists today became the prior's church and was also used by the townspeople as their parish church. In the 13th century it underwent improvements, including lead for the roof in 1246. This may also explain the rapport which seems to have developed between the prior and the brethren on one side and the parishioners on the other - most clearly seen in the episode of Prior Dawbeney (a local name) narrated above. The prior and his brethren would perhaps have lived in buildings north of the quire which were later incorporated into the former vicarage. After 1400, when the number of male religious in the community diminished and ultimately disappeared, the present abbey church would have been used solely as the parish church, which it remains today.

Such an interpretation was indeed hinted at in the 1900 controversy, but it was not then realised how significant had been the male element in the community, nor that Amesbury, as a Fontevraldine house, would have been a true double house, possessing two churches and two convents.

Pilgrims and Legends

If landed interests and material possessions contributed to the priory's wealth, there were also spiritual assets.[37] A mania for pilgrimage, rekindled by the murder of Thomas Becket in 1170, brought added prosperity to all religious communities who could claim the relics of a notable saint or martyr. Amesbury as a place of pilgrimage had St Melor; and because pilgrims were also sightseers, Amesbury could also boast Stonehenge. Legends about both were resurrected and embellished, and later an Arthurian association was strengthened by the claim that Guinevere was buried at Amesbury. The medieval legends, romantic and tendentious, still exist. As historical documents they must be largely discounted, because their intention was to impress rather than to inform. But because they drew pilgrims to Amesbury, were told and re-told, believed and wondered at, and are still believed, they have become a part of Amesbury's history.

In the previous chapter it was suggested that Melor's relics and the legend of his martyrdom arrived at Amesbury after the foundation of the first abbey. His cult was certainly well established by the time of the refoundation, as William of Malmesbury, writing at the beginning of the 12th century, believed that Melor was buried at Amesbury. Two hundred years later the bald account of the saint's martyrdom, which had originated in Brittany, had been elaborated at Amesbury and various additions were circulating which seem to have been tailored to explain the changes which took place in 1177. These fables explain how the relics were brought by itinerant priests to Amesbury, where they stuck fast to the high altar, were purchased by the abbess and remained. Later thieves stole the relics and hid them in a nearby cave, until a priest named Godric discovered them and returned them to the church. His efforts were greeted by the martyr himself, who prophesied that the building would collapse and asked that his bones once again be removed. After this was done, the building collapsed. Reading between the lines of these stories it is clear that by 1350 (when they were collected and written down) the relics were no longer to be seen at Amesbury and that the building in which they had been deposited had either collapsed, or been demolished and rebuilt. It is tempting to see in these picturesque explanations a shadow of the upheaval which occurred at the refounding in 1177, as well as the excuses of the guide who could no longer show the pilgrims the actual relics which they had come to venerate.

By the time that the Melor legends had attained their final form in the 14th century, Amesbury Priory had achieved fame as the sanctuary and resting place of royal ladies, notably Queen Eleanor of Provence, who was buried here in 1291. This repentant sinner was doubtless the model for the Guinevere immortalised by Malory, who in the *Morte d'Arthur* (completed 1469) took the veil at Amesbury and died here before Lancelot, her lover, could gallop from Glastonbury to console her. The association of Guinevere with Amesbury seems to have begun in the 14th century and continued until at least 1800, when visitors were still being shown her alleged tomb.

Three hundred years before Malory, however, Arthurian figures were already at large in the neighbourhood. In a curious medley of historical romance, fantasy and genuine folklore Geoffrey of Monmouth, the 12th century chronicler, sought to explain the mystery of Stonehenge. The principal claim of his account, that Merlin miraculously transported the Giant's Dance from Ireland, is well known and has been extensively studied, but certain lesser details shed light on the importance of the monument to the status and attractiveness of Amesbury Priory as a place of pilgrimage. In particular his claim that an abbey, or 'cloister of Ambrius', was of even greater antiquity than Stonehenge (which he alleges was built to commemorate warriors buried in the cloister) reads like an attempt by the priory to impress sightseers with its own importance. The burial of slain warriors (460 altogether) perhaps appears in the story to explain the numerous barrows of all kinds dotted around the neighbouring landscape. And the appearance of Ambrosius Aurelianus is doubtless an echo of the Ambrosbury legend (with perhaps a basis in fact) which we examined in chapter one.

Geoffrey's explanations may have satisfied medieval travellers but do not, in general, impress historians. Certain details (such as 'Ambrius') seem to be his invention, others are adaptations of earlier sources not located to Amesbury, still others embody local propaganda; apart from the speculation about Ambrosius only the notion that Stonehenge was brought from foreign parts (as indeed it was) may represent a genuine tradition, preserved in different forms and in various places, and testifying to the extraordinarily potent curiosity that has always surrounded Amesbury's most precious attraction.

Melor, Guinevere and Merlin continue to haunt Amesbury's imaginations. When Amesbury forgets its demi-gods it will have lost something very precious.

The Medieval Town

A town clustered around the gates of a famous monastery was the nearest that medieval Europe came to the 19th century industrial town, encircling the factory on which it depended. An abbey was a kind of medieval factory, employing various skills to produce the necessities of daily life. A lease of 1560[38] lists a number of buildings and operations that had been part of the former priory precinct, including barns, stables, blademills, garners, orchards, dovecots, gardens, ponds, woods, fishing and floodhatches, besides the strictly agricultural concerns. Amesbury men and women doubtless found employment here, whilst others were engaged in the service of individual members of the monastic community. A certain Pontius Florak, for instance, who lived in 1323 at a house in Pouncette Street, Amesbury, appears in another document as a bailiff of the nun Mary, daughter of Edward I.[39] Together with two accomplices, also Mary's servants, he had tried to recover possession of a house which Mary owned at Ugford, near Wilton, and his zeal had landed him in Old Sarum gaol.

Amesbury, of course, was by no means unique in the way it developed around an important monastery. In Wiltshire alone there are two other places which could tell a similar story. At Lacock, which then lay on a main highway, a small town was laid out, probably in the 1230s, at the gates of an Augustinian nunnery; and at Bradenstoke, near Lyneham, a market place and fairground developed in the 14th century along the main street to the priory, and was known as Clack. The story could be repeated in many parts of the country.

Quite apart from the prosperity which the abbey as a place of pilgrimage and employment bestowed on Amesbury, it also dominated the religious life of the town, which appears to have had no parish church apart from the present abbey church; and this, as we have suggested, was controlled by the priory, at least until 1400, either for the nuns themselves or as the prior's church. It need hardly be said that a medieval town's church was the most important and powerful institution which it possessed.

It may come as a surprise, therefore, in view of the priory's apparent domination of medieval Amesbury, to learn that until quite late in its history the prioress owned no property in the parish other than her own precinct.[40] The old royal manor of Amesbury (or Amesbury Earls as it came to be known) passed through a succession of hands in the five centuries separating the conquest from the dissolution. Lords of the Amesbury manor included members of some of the principal families of England - Lancaster, Despencer, Montagu, Nevill, Clarence - but for much of its history it was in the hands of the Earls of Salisbury, and it is to this connection that both Earls Court and Countess Court Farms owe their names. The manor of Amesbury Earls controlled by far the largest proportion of the parish. Gradually, however, from 1286 onwards, the prioress accumulated lands in Amesbury and these had, by the time of the dissolution, been grouped together to form the manor of Amesbury Priors. They mostly lay in West Amesbury. Other parcels of land in Amesbury were at various times distinguished as manors: 'The Conygar' manor, recorded in 1382, is remembered by the name Coneybury Hill in West Amesbury; another West Amesbury manor, known as 'Dawbeneys', had a protracted existence from the 13th to the 17th centuries; a house with two mills and a few acres of land in Amesbury is described as the manor of Cantilupe and may, at the time of the dissolution, have become the manor of Souths, although this is conjectural.

Much more detailed study is necessary before a full description of the agricultural and community life of Amesbury in the middle ages can be determined. Here, as elsewhere, the open field system of farming was used, the town being surrounded by enormous fields divided by baulks into furlongs which were themselves divided into long strips, or acres. Two or three fields belonged to each manor, and were cultivated in rotation, to allow a period of fallow. Most households who were not employed by the priory or engaged in a trade, as well as many who were, would have worked their acres in the fields, at first as villeins, unfree servants of the lord of the manor, whose condition was little better than slavery, but later in the medieval period as free tenants of the lord. A few would have been directly employed by the lord to farm the demesne land of the manor, and all would have been required to render service from time to time on the lord's land. From the Antrobus Deeds we may glimpse this system at work, especially in the common fields of West Amesbury, which formed the priory lands. A document in 1397[41] refers to three fields - West, South and East - and the first of these, West Field, seems to have survived intact until 18th century enclosure. It was bordered by Coneybury Hill on the north and the parish boundary on the south. South Field lay across the river from West Amesbury; by 1612 it was being known as South Ham Field and in the Flitcroft Atlas of 1726 it is divided into Little and Great South Ham Fields. East Field does not recur after 1479, but instead two other fields in West Amesbury are mentioned, Middle Field, which lay to the north of Coneybury Hill, and Half Borough Field, which lay to the west of Vespasian's Camp ('borough' refers to the hillfort). Individual tenants farmed acres dotted haphazardly within the furlongs which made up these fields, so that each had his share of good and bad land. The fields of Amesbury town also figure in the Antrobus Deeds, although less prominently and mostly after the dissolution. Thus we have Barnard Field (1602) in the area of the Boscombe Down complex, Black Cross Field (1612) east of the main road to Salisbury,

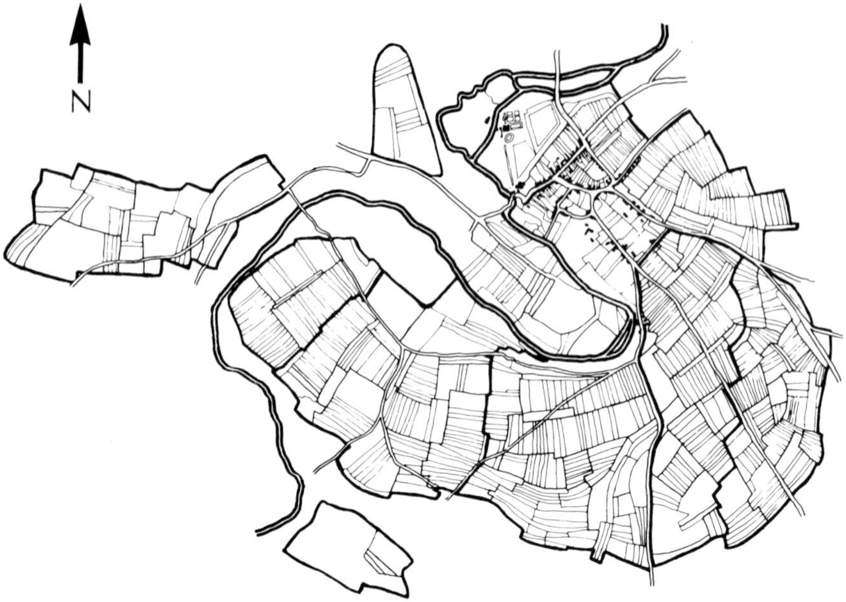
N

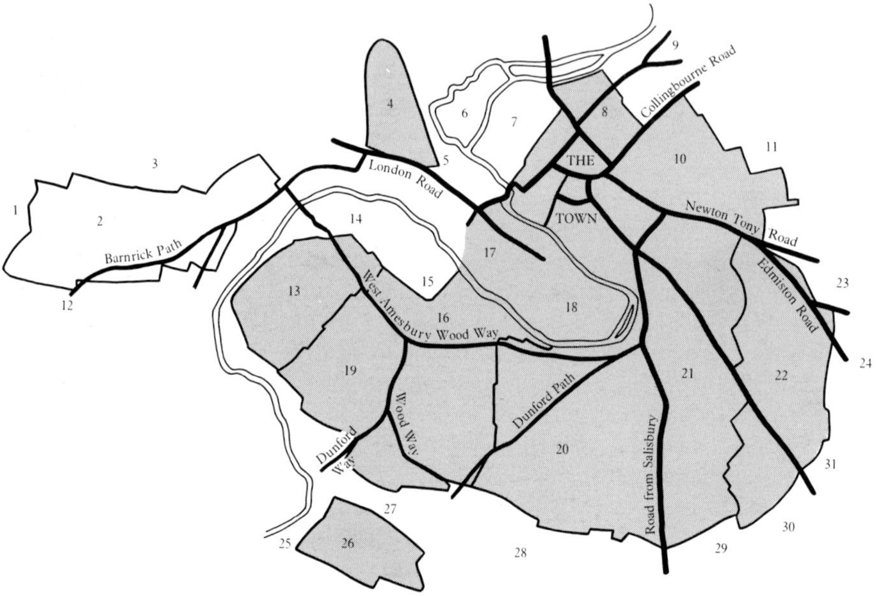
1
2
3
4
5
6
7
8
9
10
11
12
13
14
15
16
17
18
19
20
21
22
23
24
25
26
27
28
29
30
31
Collingbourne Road
London Road
THE
TOWN
Newton Tony Road
Edmiston Road
Barnrick Path
West Amesbury Wood Way
Wood Way
Dunford Way
Dunford Path
Road from Salisbury

THE COMMON FIELDS OF AMESBURY IN 1726

The two maps opposite show the common fields of Amesbury divided into furlongs and acres (top) and the principal fields, roads and trackways (bottom) as they appear on the 'Book of Mapps' by Henry Flitcroft, commissioned by the third duke of Queensberry in 1726.

1 Abbey Down
2 West Field
3 Middle Field
4 Walls Field
5 Pit Fall Hill
6 Laundry Mead
7 The Demesne
8 Town End Little Field
9 Ratfin Farm
10 Cuckold's Hill Field
11 Earl's Farm Middle Field and Lower Field
12 Normanton Lordship
13 Little South Ham Field
14 Cow Leas
15 South Ham Closes
16 Goose Land Furlong
17 Little Field over the Water
18 Wet and Dry Whitnams
19 Great South Ham Field
20 South Mill Hill Field
21 Bartnett Field
22 Black Cross Field
23 Earl's Farm Upper Field
24 Town Down
25 Pidgeon Hill
26 Woolson Hill Field
27 Woolson Hill Down
28 Lower Down
29 Vinons Farm Down
30 Kickdom Down
31 Black Cross Down

Only the occasional rusting hatchway and derelict watercourses remain of the once complex water-meadow system.

South Middle Field or South Mill Hill Field (1692, 1612) west of the Salisbury road, Town End Little Field (1613) on the site of Coldharbour and the Antrobus Road estate, and Countess Field (1502) to the north of Amesbury. Other fields also existed on the land later occupied by Earls Court Farm, and at Ratfyn Farm, which had always been quite separate from Amesbury.

In addition to the main concern of farming the arable land a variety of animals was reared. Cattle and sheep manured the arable land in winter or when left fallow, and grazed the downs and the meadows in summer. Sheep might be owned either by the lord of the manor, whose flock at Amesbury ran into thousands, or by individual tenant farmers who would pay for a shepherd in common. Amesbury's sheep flock was so large in 1295 that extra labour had to be hired for the shearing. Horses and oxen were bred for work; pigs and rabbits supplemented the meagre diet. Perhaps typical of the Amesbury tenant farmer in the middle ages were John and Christine Balet, whose farm in 1497 consisted of one messuage (farmhouse), half a virgate of land (perhaps about six hectares), two acres of meadow (less than one hectare), pasture for one horse and five oxen, 50 sheep, two rams and ten pigs.[42]

In its method of agriculture Amesbury was no different from villages throughout much of the country. As a small town, however, it had attributes not shared by its neighbours. We have seen that it was the eponymous centre of local administration, the hundred, which was in 1334 the second most prosperous hundred in Wiltshire. The lord of its principal manor derived various benefits from being also the lord of the hundred. It was a judicial centre as well, the venue for hundred courts, in addition to the local manorial courts leet and baron, by which the common fields were managed and wrongdoers taken to task. It seems also to have aspired for a time to the status of a borough, since a deed of 1314 talks of Thomas Pertuht, burgess of Amesbury;[43] but Amesbury never actually became a borough. Most important of all to Amesbury's prosperity was that it possessed a weekly market. The earliest Amesbury market grant to be identified was made to William Longspee, Earl of Salisbury in 1252, and it was probably confirmed in 1268/9. It was for a Thursday market, but it had probably lapsed by the 14th century, for in 1317 we find the prioress being granted a Saturday market, and it was this that endured. Annual fairs were also the subject of the 1252 and later royal grants, the most important of which was held on 6th May, a date associated with St Melor.[44] This trading function, besides allowing the manors to sell their surplus produce, enabled specialist skills and crafts to develop in the town. According to the Antrobus Deeds a carpenter, baker, washerwoman, fleshmonger, merchant, draper, cobbler, tailor, leatherworker and chandler all existed in medieval or Tudor Amesbury.

One important effect of Amesbury's transition from a Saxon royal estate centre to a small but busy medieval town must have been the development of its street plan. How and when this occurred remain matters for conjecture, but it would be reasonable to connect the laying out of Salisbury Street as a broad market place (it was narrowed and disguised again in the 19th century) with the establishment of an official market in the 13th century. Town planning of this kind was occurring all over England at this time, and in south Wiltshire alone Downton, Hindon, Mere and Heytesbury were all in the process of being transformed into small towns. The creation and rapid expansion of Salisbury, the new town par excellence, was also taking place at the same period.

A number of the streets of medieval Amesbury are known by name. Salisbury Street, first mentioned in 1551,[45] is the only one to bear its present name. High Street was formerly known as Marlborough Street, a name still in use as late as 1816;[46] via Ratfyn Road it connected with the Old Marlborough Road through Bulford and Everleigh, which until the 19th century would have been used as the way to Marlborough in preference to the modern route beginning in Countess Road. Frog Lane (now part of Flower Lane) occurs in a document of 1463, and two unidentified streets, Carpenter Street (perhaps named after an individual called Carpenter rather than implying a street of carpenters) and Pouncette Street, occur as early as 1321 and 1323.[47] It is clear from the context that Carpenter Street ran roughly north-south, and so it may be an early name for the road which later became Back Lane and is now School Lane. *Pouncettestret* or *Pouncestes Strete* seems to refer to Pancet, or Penchet, an old name for Clarendon Forest, with which the Saxon estate, and later the medieval priory, had connections. Smithfield Street does not occur in medieval documents, although it must have existed from an early date; it may be a corruption of South Ham Field Street, which is where it led. Since, as we have seen, it was the manor of Amesbury Earls, rather than the priory, which owned and controlled much of the parish, it would be reasonable to expect a second focus of settlement around the lord of the manor's demesne house and farm. Where this might have been in the middle ages is unknown, but building debris and foundations which survived until the 19th century south of Flower Lane, near Vineys Farm, could well have been connected with it.[48]

Archaeology alone can now recover details of the buildings which once lined the medieval streets. We know that there were three inns - the Three Cups in Marlborough Street, the present George (probably 15th century although the earliest documentary reference is 1560) and the Swan (perhaps on the site of the present Bell Hotel). We have too a description of a piece of redevelopment in 1474:[49]

> Lease indented for 40 years by Robert Saucer to William Clarke of Great Ambresbur' and Margaret his wife of a tenement with a garden in Marleborghstrete between the tenement of the lessees called le yatehous and the tenement of the prioress and convent... The lessees covenant to build the tenement anew in manner fit for dwelling in, as in hall, chamber, shop and solar, with all parcloses [partitions], keep them in repair at their own expense and so repaired to leave them.

Estimates of medieval population must be made with very great caution. In the previous chapter we suggested that the population of Amesbury in 1086 may have been about 700. During the next 250 years no figures are available, but it appears that the population of Wiltshire generally, as elsewhere, grew quite significantly.[50] A tax assessment of 1334 suggests that Amesbury, or certain individuals in the town at least, had become quite prosperous. Taking together the assessments for Great Amesbury, Amesbury Priors and West Amesbury, the wealth of Amesbury was exceeded by only six places in Wiltshire - Salisbury, Chippenham, Bremhill, Corsham, Wanborough and Donhead. It would perhaps be reasonable to guess that Amesbury's population had risen, by the year of the Black Death, 1348, to about 1,000. The effect of the Black Death on Amesbury is not known, but at neighbouring Durrington 18 out of 41 holdings had fallen vacant by 1349. A similar casualty rate at Amesbury may be reflected in the poll tax return of 1377, which gives an adjusted figure of about 600 for the total population. Nonetheless, Amesbury was still more populous than most Wiltshire communities, including boroughs, and was surpassed only by Salisbury, Wilton, Melksham, Mere, Marlborough and Malmesbury.

The Dissolution

The dissolution, by Henry VIII, of every surviving monastery in the land during the decade 1530-40 is commonly misconceived as a religious act, part and parcel of the reformation of the English church and the estrangement from Rome.[51] In practice it was also an attempt to redistribute the ownership of land throughout the country to private magnates at the expense of the largely inactive and spiritually redundant monastic estates. The stark remains of ruined abbeys suggest a brutality in the dissolution which is misleading; in general the process was achieved with due regard for the welfare of the dispossessed inmates, an adherence to the letter of the law, and only muted opposition. However, the implications of the disappearance of the abbey for Amesbury after nearly six centuries were enormous and far-reaching; they mark the end of a chapter of the town's history and a new beginning.

Dissolution, at first sporadic and then, from 1536, concentrated on the smaller communities, reached its peak in the years 1538 and 1539, when every monastery, even mighty Glastonbury, found itself under threat of closure. The prioress of Amesbury, Florence Bonnewe, was visited by two commissioners on 29th March 1539, who hoped to take immediate possession of the convent, as they had recently done at Shaftesbury and Wilton and some 40 houses altogether. Florence Bonnewe, however, sided with the minority of monastic heads who resisted, whether from a genuine distaste for the proceedings, or merely in order to buy time for her nuns to make suitable arrangements for their welfare. Her refusal to accept a pension and her offer to resign suggest the former. However, by her stand she earned a respite for her house for eight months, until 4th December 1539. By then her resignation had been obtained and a new, more compliant prioress appointed. This was Joan Darrell, after Florence Bonnewe probably the most senior and respectable member of the convent. She surrendered her house, one of the last monasteries in the country to yield to dissolution, and received a pension, along with the 33 nuns still residing at Amesbury. With her surrender the priory of Amesbury was brought to an end.

Chapter 4

Landlord, Tenant, and Land

The Squire

To the inhabitants of Amesbury in 1540 it must have seemed as if the end of the world had come.[52] The old order, dominated by the priory, was taken apart stone by stone and carted away by merchants for use elsewhere; Amesbury found itself under the control of a secular lord, Edward Seymour, then Earl of Hertford and later Protector Somerset. In place of the venerable monastery, with its pilgrims and legends, there now arose a gentleman's seat, constructed out of the only parts of the priory deemed worthy of preservation - the hall, buttery, pantry and kitchen. Seymour was more powerful in Amesbury than the prioress had ever been. Not only did he hold the manor of Amesbury Priory, which was granted to him in 1541, but also the other important manor, that of Amesbury Earls, which the crown had granted him in 1536 in preparation for the dissolution. Thus for the first time since the Saxon period virtually the whole of Amesbury was under the control of a single owner, and so it remained until the manorial system lost its influence in the 19th century.

The Seymour family retained the Amesbury manors through successive generations until 1675, in which year John Seymour, 4th Duke of Somerset, died without issue. There were, it is true, precarious moments in the Seymour tenure. For a few years in the 1550s the property was confiscated by the crown, and between 1611 and 1615 the rightful owner, Sir William Seymour, was in exile in France. However, there is plenty of evidence that members of the Seymour family spent considerable periods in residence at Amesbury, during which they built the two surviving lodges, Kent House and Diana House, and after 1660 the first purpose-built mansion, the precursor of the present Amesbury Abbey. Whilst it is true that the family was important in the social life of the nation, having produced patrons of the arts and great beauties (for one of whom a rejected lover committed suicide in an Amesbury inn after writing a love song in his own blood), and whilst it is also true that Seymours held some of the highest offices in the land, it must be confessed that, of all the principal owners of Amesbury, they seem to have contributed least to the life of the town.

The estate passed by marriage to the Bruce family, who retained it for some 40 years, 1676-1720, before selling it to a prominent statesman, Lord Carleton. Carleton's fondness for avenues is preserved in 'Lord's Walk', but he cannot have lived to see his lime trees reach maturity, since he died after a mere five years at Amesbury in 1725. Carleton bequeathed the manors of Amesbury to his nephew

Charles, 3rd Duke of Queensberry, and Amesbury appears to have embarked on an eventful era under a squire more than usually enlightened to the civic duties which his privileged position ought to entail.

Queensberry and his wife Catherine (or 'Kitty') were forceful characters and influential members of fashionable society. They incurred the wrath of the court over their patronage of the poet John Gay, who is traditionally, but wrongly, believed to have written the Beggar's Opera in an artificial 'cave' in the abbey grounds - in fact the land on which the cave was built was not acquired by the Queensberrys until years after the opera's publication.[53] Kitty and her husband defiantly welcomed their ostracism from court and became the talk of the noble circles in which they moved by making Amesbury a fashionable alternative for high society. During their long association with the town, which ended with the duke's death in 1778, Amesbury underwent changes, some dramatic, some insidious, such as seldom occur in the life of a community. These changes, the disastrous fires of 1745 and 1751, the process of enclosure of the common fields, the inauguration of the turnpike trust and the building of Queensberry Bridge, will be discussed in their proper places, but it is important to realise that they all took place within 30 years of each other, and behind each project and improvement may be seen the hand of Queensberry. By egalitarian modern standards the duke's elaborate gardens, fine house and lavish entertainments may suggest shallow generosity to the squalid tenants who surrounded him; but even if stories of Kitty's charity are apocryphal - she apparently furnished her cottagers with specially designed warm snug chairs of straw - the 3rd Duke and Duchess of Queensberry were no worse than many of their contemporaries, and immeasurably better than their successor.

In 1778, when the duke died without surviving issue, the Amesbury estate passed to his cousin, William Douglas, who thereby became the 4th Duke of Queensberry. Few kind words have been written about 'Old Q', as he was known, and it is most unlikely that any passed the lips of his Amesbury tenants between his arrival in 1778 and his death in 1810. By all accounts his chief interest in Amesbury, after he had removed everything of value to furnish his new house in Richmond,[54] lay in the price he might obtain by selling it, and this became, if the turnpike accounts are typical, one of the preoccupations of his life. He was successful in renting the mansion for short periods during his prolonged absences, notably from 1794-1800 to a group of refugee nuns from Louvain, but by the time of his death the fine Webb house had fallen into such disrepair that almost total rebuilding was necessary. The town, too, according to a writer in 1801, had "all the appearance of decay," its inhabitants remembering with fondness Old Q's predecessors, and repining, "that the rents collected from the produce of their industry are spent in distant neighbourhoods, or swallowed up in the prodigal vices of a large city."[55]

'Old Q' died a bachelor, and the estate was ultimately put up for sale. The buyer, in 1824, was Sir Edmund Antrobus. Members of the Antrobus family remained and remain lords of the manor, although the mansion was sold in 1979 to become a nursing home. Undoubtedly the squirearchy, as represented by Sir

Edmund, continued to be a potent force in local society throughout the 19th century and into the 20th. To commemorate Queen Victoria's coronation, for instance, Sir Edmund and Lady Antrobus provided a meal of roast beef, plum pudding and strong beer for 500 of Amesbury's labouring population. It was probably the most substantial meal that some of them ever had in their lives. Comparable generosity was shown by later Antrobuses to mark the same queen's diamond jubilee. In the present century we have Antrobus House, Antrobus Road and the Antrobus Arms Hotel to keep alive an otherwise defunct loyalty.

Such have been the landlords of Amesbury, famous and infamous, good and bad. Because they shaped Amesbury's past their history is the history of the town. But the squire was only one out of a thousand inhabitants and his mansion only one out of 200 dwellings. His tenants also deserve their place in the history of the town.

The Tenants

The ordinary people of Victorian Amesbury are not listed in the directories, and their names are not inscribed on memorials in the parish church.[56] To all intents and purposes they are forgotten. And yet the biography of any one of them, if it could be written, would be quite as interesting as that of a Queensberry or an Antrobus. Rather than generalise, therefore, about the labouring poor of Amesbury over several centuries, we shall focus on a single year, 1851, the year of a census and, so far as we can tell, a fairly typical year in the life of 19th century Amesbury. We shall consider the whole population under this heading of 'tenants' because, although by no means everybody was the tenant of the squire, Sir Edmund Antrobus, most were, and those artisans, tradesmen and professional people who were not, nonetheless depended on his tenants for their livelihood.

The population of Amesbury in 1851 was 1,172, less than one quarter of the present total. Most of the inhabitants lived within 300 yards of the market place. Those who did not dwelt in cottages near one of the farms, West Amesbury, Countess, Ratfyn or at South Mill. The 83 least fortunate members of society existed at the workhouse built some 14 years earlier on South Mill Hill. Repeated fires had changed the face of Amesbury, but the town had expanded hardly at all during the previous 150 years; in fact the population had probably been greater two centuries earlier.[57] The people were much the same too. Nearly two-thirds of the population alive in 1851 had been born in Amesbury; only one in ten had come from further afield than south Wiltshire or nearby parts of Hampshire. A mere 18 inhabitants had not been born in England south of the Thames. Consequently there was a great deal of intermarriage between Amesbury families, so that few of the indigenous population cannot have been related, however distantly, to one another. A further consequence was that certain surnames were extremely common: nearly one-fifth of the population was called Truckle, Rattue, Pike, Cooper, Eyres or Mundy. Other local names were Rolfe, Asher, Kilford and Spredbury. It is pleasing to note that descendants of many of these Amesbury families are still prominent in local affairs.

The population in 1851 was a great deal younger than it is today. Fewer than one in twelve had attained the age of 60, only 32 had reached 70 and a mere four survived into their 80s. There was no reward for the elderly at the end of a hard life. William Pike, aged 72, was still employed as a shepherd, but when you could no longer work you became a pauper, and if you could not depend on the charity of relations, you went to the workhouse. Patience Rushworth, at 88 Amesbury's oldest resident, was fortunate in that she lived with her nephew, a shepherd, and his family; Mary Rawlings, however, a spinster from Enford, 82 years old, could look forward only to a pauper's death in the workhouse where she lived.

At the top of the social scale were the parson, the physicians and the farmers. Fulwar W Fowle, perpetual curate, and the longest-serving of Amesbury's priests, lived well. To minister to the needs of himself, his wife, his two unmarried daughters (the elder of independent means) and his 18-year-old son (described as "scholar-at-home") he employed four house servants, all local girls. Twice during his incumbency (in 1824 and 1859) he applied to extend the parsonage house to accommodate his ample household. The surgeon, George Best Batho, and the general practitioner, Charles Pyle, both employed servants, and the latter seems to have run a small school for young ladies in his house, for whom he employed two governesses. Perhaps the wealthiest of all the upper-class residents was Robert Pinckney, who two years earlier had sold his tenancy of West Amesbury Farm, and now in his early 50s lived in retirement with his wife and daughter, four servants and a footman, in the house which has become the Antrobus Arms Hotel. Likewise Joseph Purnell, whose mother had run the George Inn and who had himself farmed the park lands of the abbey, in 1851 was living in comfortable retirement on an annuity with his housekeeper, his butler and a domestic servant. The active farmers, too, could afford large households: Thomas Tanner (Earls Court Farm) employed a governess for his four children, a cook, a groom and two servants; Edmund Olding (Ratfyn Farm) and Henry Selfe (Countess Farm) had three servants apiece; and Ann Long (Red House and Viney's Farm) had four; even Michael Rooke, the 29-year-old farmer of West Amesbury, employed two house servants for himself and his young wife. Altogether the monied classes of Amesbury provided employment for about 60 domestic servants, nearly all of whom were unmarried women in their teens or twenties.

Inferior to these petty gentry were the master craftsmen and businessmen of Amesbury. It was their presence, some 30 in all, with their own premises independent of the squire and their own employees, which marked Amesbury out as a town among the surrounding villages. None of these industries was very large: Joseph Sandell, tailor and glover, had nine employees; Edwin Andrews, carpenter, employed five men and one apprentice; Joseph Olding, miller at South Mill, employed four. Many craftsmen had a single employee or none at all. Some employed only apprentices, and these might lodge with their master; such were Joseph Gane, a blacksmith, and William Eyers, boot and shoemaker. In other cases the family business was maintained by the late craftsman's widow; thus Elizabeth Cread was a carpenter employing five men, and Mary Turner a blacksmith with three employees. Fanny Gilbert, 73, was a "mistress plumber". Those businessmen who prospered might aspire to a domestic servant, but few could afford more than one. Others, such as Joseph Hillary, a tailor, needed to supplement the family's income by whatever wife and daughter could earn as laundresses, sempstresses or glovers.

Relatively few inhabitants, apart from domestic servants, were employed in what today would be called service industries. There were a number of teachers, mostly unmarried schoolmistresses or governesses; there were the toll-gate keepers, the staff of the workhouse, the shopkeepers, the publicans, and James Maggs, the sole police officer. There were also the staff of the Amesbury Abbey estate - gamekeeper, gardeners and grooms. However, these altogether amounted to no more than one in twenty of the population.

Beneath the minor professional people and craftsmen were the men and women who worked for them. Usually styled 'journeymen' they seem to have enjoyed a higher standard of living than their counterpart wage-earners who worked in the fields. In several instances two or more journeymen living together could afford a domestic servant; others were able to support large families; still others were lodgers or younger members of a family, for whom an apprenticeship had enabled them to better themselves. Perhaps one-twelfth of the population was employed as journeymen or apprentices.

Next in the social order came the largest category of all, those who were, or were dependent upon, farm labourers. The number of labourers employed by the respective farms was as follows: Earls Farm, 71; Countess Farm, 53; Red House Farm, 39; West Amesbury Farm, 29; Ratfyn Farm, 28. All but the last of these farms was owned by Sir Edmund Antrobus, and so the vast majority of labourers worked land which belonged to the squire. However expert they may have been at the crafts of husbandry, most farmworkers boasted no particular skill (to the census enumerator at least), their duties dictated by the seasons and their masters. There were those who specialised, however, a carter, two dairymen and no fewer than 15 shepherds. Charles Purdue and John Blake, labourer and ploughboy respectively, were the youngest farmworkers. a mere eight years apiece. Many wives and daughters also worked in the fields alongside their menfolk. The number of farm labourers was equalled by the number of their dependants, and altogether this social class included four out of every ten of the population. They were the least mobile of all; all but a handful had been born within a morning's walk of Amesbury. Many farmworkers had large families, with six or more surviving children; George Pike and his wife, both aged 38, had eight children, aged between 17 years and one month, living at home, but the record for dependants was held by his neighbour, Moses Truckle, who at a mere 33 had accumulated four children, three nieces, one wife, one nephew and one mother-in-law. To offset their more prolific colleagues, however, it should be noted that many labourers were bachelors lodging with families, or were younger members of a household. On average the Amesbury farm labourer's family was not much larger than the average family today.

By 1851 very few children were not receiving formal education for five years or longer. The schools which existed to cater for their needs will be discussed in a later chapter; here it will suffice to comment on the pattern of school attendance. Most boys began school when they were four and continued until they were at least eight, and usually ten; few stayed longer, as they were required to work in the fields or, if they were clever, they might be apprenticed to a trade. Girls, on the other hand, usually stayed at home until they were six, and then attended school at least until they were ten, and many remained until they were 13. Many would then be employed in domestic service for a period before becoming wives and mothers. Exactly 200 schoolchildren are listed in Amesbury in the 1851 census, with another 35 attending the school in the workhouse.

At the bottom of the social scale came the paupers, with no visible means of support. The more fortunate among them, about 30 in Amesbury, retained their freedom and a little of their dignity by remaining in the community, living with relatives or in the cottages where they had spent much of their lives. A few were perhaps able-bodied but idle, but most were incapable of earning their keep through old age or infirmity. When survival became impossible their only recourse was to the workhouse. The catalogue of names of the 83 inmates in 1851 reminds us of a side of Victorian life which we might prefer to forget. Here were to be found the elderly whose partners were dead, orphans left to fend for themselves in a cruel world and, most depressing of all, the infant children of unmarried mothers. Such was Ann Viney, conceived seven years earlier by a 19-year-old washerwoman, born in the workhouse, and now joined by a brother, three months old but without a name as yet. He, and the three other unnamed workhouse babies, were a far cry from the squire and the vicar, the surgeon and the farmer, though each took his place within the society of Victorian Amesbury.

Agriculture

Until the arrival of military establishments in the 20th century, agriculture was the mainstay of Amesbury's economy and the principal occupation, as we have seen, of the largest group of the town's inhabitants. Before about 1750 the pattern of agriculture had changed little for centuries, the large common fields still being known by their medieval names and still divided into furlongs and acres. This is shown by the magnificent Flitcroft maps of the fields of Amesbury in 1726[58] and by various surveys. In an extent of 1502, for instance,[59] the following fields are mentioned: *Countes Fyld, Westfilld, Gret Ambr' Fild, Hawborow Fyld, Suthamme, Lytull Ambresbury Fild, Normanton Fild*. Other documents of 1602 and 1612 refer to *Barnard Fild, the Myddle Fielde and Blackecrossefield*; nearly all these names appear on Flitcroft's maps and in a survey of 1742.[60] The names of furlongs and acres endured in similar fashion for centuries until enclosure in the 18th century swept them away.

Enclosure, the process whereby the large medieval common fields were divided into smaller, enclosed areas under the control of a single tenant, was not carried out at Amesbury, as in many places, by Act of Parliament, and so cannot be pinned down to a single date. Since virtually the whole of Amesbury was controlled by one landowner, the Duke of Queensberry, he was free to enclose his land piecemeal without legal sanction, and the process may have taken some years to complete. As a result its achievement was perhaps less traumatic to the smaller tenants than in other parishes, where enclosure was imposed at a single date by Act of Parliament. It is clear that the majority of the manor was enclosed between 1742 and 1771; the survey of 1742 records every piece of enclosed land at that date, but with the exceptions of Northams and Southams Closes the only enclosures were gardens, orchards and meads, few larger than one or two acres. By 1771, however,[61] most land owned by the manor had been divided between six farms, in order of size, Red House Farm, South Ham Farm, Earls Farm, Countess Court Farm, West Amesbury Farm, and Kent House Farm. These six, together with the abbey mansion, controlled 5,105 acres of pasture, meadowland, arable and downland. Fifty years later, in 1824,[62] although the total acreage remained about the same, several changes had occurred. The number of farms had been reduced to four, by the incorporation of South Ham into Red House Farm and parts of Kent House (or Park) into Countess and West Amesbury Farms; the proportion of land under cultivation (2,670 acres) was now slightly more than half the total, whereas in 1771 it had been only one-third; and the acreage of maiden down, that is downland never cultivated, had been reduced from 2,514 to 2,056 acres. This pattern is confirmed by an examination of the tithe award for 1841[63] which shows that nearly all the parish south of Boscombe Road and the river was farmed by William Long of Red House Farm, the land between Boscombe Road and London Road by Thomas Tanner of Earls Farm, West Amesbury and everything south of the present Exeter Road by Robert Pinckney of West Amesbury Farm, and most of the remainder, that is land to the north and east of Stonehenge across Countess Road to the river, by Henry Selfe of Countess Farm. A fifth farmer, Edmund Olding, occupied Ratfyn Farm with 500 acres north of London Road, but this land did not form part of the Amesbury manor.

Enclosure was in part responsible for the increased efficiency of agriculture in Amesbury in the 19th century, which lasted until the great agricultural depression of the 1870s. A second factor was the gradual introduction of machinery. One such machine, for winnowing corn, invented by a certain John Trowbridge, was apparently named 'The Amesbury Heaver', but nothing further appears to be known about this invention.[64] The agricultural labourers, already impoverished by enclosure and depressed wages, did not wish to know about such machines, which posed a further threat to their livelihood, and their concern took the form of a series of incendiary attacks at various places in the winter of 1830/1, including two incidents at Countess Farm.[65] Mechanisation does not, however, appear to have resulted in an exodus from the land around Amesbury, as the population of the parish increased from 723 in 1811 to 1,065 in 1841 (excluding the inmates of the workhouse) and thence remained steady until the 1890s.

A third improvement which took place from the 17th to the 19th centuries

32

THE TOWN OF AMESBURY IN 1726

The town survey from the 1726 Flitcroft book of maps, which records the traditional common fields prior to enclosure - a system of agriculture little changed since medieval times. An examination of the original map provides a fascinating insight into Amesbury's character in the early 18th century. Although the basic layout of the town's central area was similar to that of today, the importance and names of some thoroughfares differed from the present. Salisbury Street did not exist as such; its northern half was the market place, wider than today, and with its market house at the junction with High Street; its southern half was Smithfield Street, which continued round to its junction with Cold Harbour. Part of Flower Lane, then called Frog Lane, ran from the river to the market place, earlier providing access to the town from the west. Today's Salisbury Road was South Mill Lane and continued as such from its junction with Smithfield Street, along its full length to South Mill. The present Earls Court Road was named Baker's Lane, and School Lane was Back Lane. Other points to note are Church Street and the staggered junction of High Street and London Road. The former gives access to the church, West Mill and the river, and to the other large buildings close by, which may well have been associated with the former priory. Population appears to have been concentrated mainly along Church Street, High Street and the Market Place, thinning out towards South Mill Lane, Baker's Lane and Cold Harbour. Small fields, paddocks and extensive orchards existed close to the town centre. The characteristic strips of land cultivated by tenants can be seen in the 'Little Field Over The Water', which corresponds approximately to the cemetery and recreation ground area today. The naming of fields is also of interest, with 'Paradice Mead' and 'Hell' existing uneasily close together by the river near the church.

concerned the irrigation of water meadows by a system of artificial watercourses controlled by hatches.[66] King's Island Hatches, Bowles Hatches, Ham Hatches and Moor Hatches, all within Amesbury parish, are reminders of the system which, by the controlled flooding of a large area of meadowland, produced a grass crop earlier in the spring than had hitherto been possible. This enabled more sheep to be kept, which in turn led to more fertile soil for the principal crops of

A common sight in former years - large flocks of sheep being driven between pastures or to the annual sheepfair. This flock is in Countess Road in the 1920's.

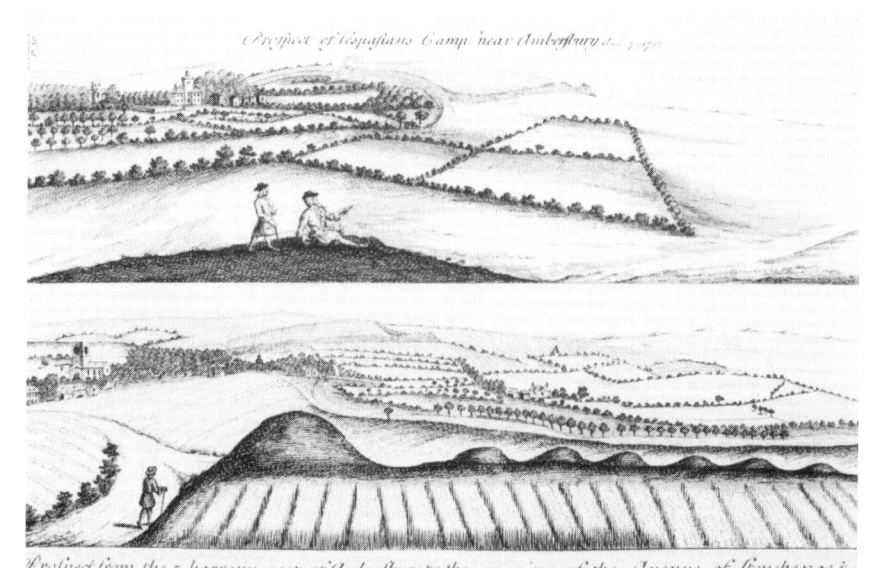

Two engravings by William Stukeley, published in 1723. The buildings to the right of the Abbey Mansion in the upper illustration may be remnants of monastic buildings. Large open fields can be seen alongside recently enclosed downland.

wheat and barley, since the chief value of sheep to the farmer was as a source of manure. This system of farming, involving large flocks of sheep and extensive 'drowning' of watermeadows, persisted until traditional agriculture was ruined by bad harvests and foreign competition towards the end of the last century.

The relationship between the squire, the tenant and the land was, in the view of many, a triangle of exploitation, subservience and hatred. John Britton, in 1801, commented on the three or four "agricultural canibals" in the neighbourhood of Amesbury, "who have devoured their eight or ten families apiece."[67] And William Cobbett saw Amesbury at first hand during his journey down the Avon valley in 1826, four years before the agricultural riots, and although political overtones colour his account, it is worth quoting nevertheless:

> If, when a wagon-load of wheat goes off [to market] in the morning, the wagon came back at night loaded with cloth, salt, or something or other, equal in value to the wheat, except what might be necessary to leave with the shopkeeper as his profit; then, indeed, the people might see the wagon go off without tears in their eyes. But now they see it go to carry away, and to bring next to nothing in return...I see it with pleasure that the common people know that they are ill-used and that they cordially, most cordially, hate those who ill-treat them.[68]

Chapter 5

The Trading Town (1539-1914)

The Clay Pipe Industry

The manufacture of clay pipes in England followed closely upon the introduction of tobacco in about 1570 and continued until the present century. At first concentrated on the large cities, such as London and Bristol, it had spread, by 1600, to most parts of the country, small manufacturers springing up to serve a local area wherever there was a supply of clay suitable for pipe manufacture. Use was very often made of known quarries which had previously been used for the white slip applied to certain medieval pottery. The manufacture of pipes was a skilful and elaborate series of processes, which depended for its success on the careful preparation of the clay, shaping by hand and with a mould, and firing in a kiln for a period of as long as 15 hours.

In the 17th century Amesbury was an important centre for the manufacture of clay pipes, and the quality of its products became famous far beyond the local needs which it supplied.[69] The industry at Amesbury seems to have been confined fairly closely to the 17th century; the earliest known example of a 'Fox' pipe (believed to have been made at Amesbury) dates from ca.1600, and the latest known maker, Gabriel Bayley, who took over the Gauntlet business in 1698, seems to have disappeared from the town by 1726.

The names of four pipe-makers' firms believed to have been working at Amesbury are recorded, although the precise dates of their activity and their whereabouts are uncertain. First comes Edward Fox, whose pipes, embellished with the emblem of a fox on their heels, have been found at Salisbury and Devizes (although it is not certain that he worked in Amesbury). Robert Smith, a pipe-maker at Amesbury in 1664, is known from documentary evidence. Gabriel Bayley, who produced in 1698 a very fine pipe to celebrate his acquisition of the Gauntlet business, does not appear to have survived for long.

The pipe-making industry at Amesbury, however, is primarily associated with the Gauntlet family.[70] The earliest reference found to a Gauntlet at Amesbury is in 1599, and thence throughout the 17th century the name is prominent in local affairs. Two early writers speak favourably of Gauntlet pipes: Aubrey calls them "the best tobacco pipes in England", and Fuller the best for shape and colour.[71] In 1651 the Duke of Bedford ordered a gross of clay pipes for 18/6 (£0.93p) from Hugh Gauntlet at the sign of the Swan, Amesbury, and this appears to have been a regular order. Clay pipe-makers regularly used an emblem stamped on the heel of the pipe to denote their products, and the Gauntlet's family mark, the palm of a hand, or gauntlet, became such a guarantee of quality that it was taken up and pirated by manufacturers in many parts of the country, especially after the Gauntlet family had ceased trading. A lawsuit is recorded by the Gauntlets against one of their imitators, which was dismissed on the technicality that the imitator had portrayed a left hand instead of the right hand used by the Gauntlets. Thus the occurrence of a gauntlet on the heel of a pipe does not necessarily denote that the pipe was a genuine Amesbury product; it is nevertheless a compliment to the high esteem in which Amesbury pipes were held that they should find imitators throughout the country.

The site of the Gauntlets' manufactory is not now known. In the Duke of Bedford's order quoted above it appears that Hugh Gauntlet was connected with the Swan Inn. Aubrey states that the clay for the pipes was brought from Chitterne, and whilst there must be truth in this - Aubrey was personally acquainted with members of the Gauntlet family - there were doubtless also more local supplies, which attracted the industry to Amesbury in the first place. According to a local tradition recorded by Kemm and perhaps dating back to 1700 the manufactory was sited between West Amesbury and Normanton, just outside the boundary of the Priory manor at a place known as Wrestler's Gate, and that the pipe-clay was dug on the site.[72] As recently as 1880 a pit at Amesbury was being pointed out as the site of the pipe-clay quarry; its precise location is not recorded, although there is a widespread belief current today that pipes were manufactured in the vicinity of Comilla House, north of the High Street.

Turnpikes and Stagecoaches

Whether through missed opportunities or inhospitable surroundings, Amesbury's career as a roadside town has been less successful than is often imagined.[73] It is true that until recently derelict petrol stations testified to the traffic (now by-passed) of recent years, just as the George Inn and the former New Inn (Comilla House) conjure up the busy stagecoaches of the 1830s, but, these two eras apart, the daunting journey across Salisbury Plain seems to have deterred all but the most intrepid of travellers. Amesbury never developed along the Exeter Road in the way that Marlborough (a town of comparable situation) developed along the Bath Road.

Roads in general in 1700 were worse than at any time since prehistory. Traffic increased yearly whilst the means of repair, statute labour organised by the parish vestry, remained as half-hearted and inept as ever. Parishes such as Amesbury, which lay on or near main highways, suffered a disproportionate burden compared with isolated neighbouring villages, whose roads were seldom used by any but their own inhabitants. Turnpiking, whereby a group of trustees took over the responsibility for a stretch of road in return for the right to collect tolls from it, came to Wiltshire in 1706, and to Amesbury at the height of the turnpike movement in 1762. By an Act of Parliament of that year the Amesbury Turnpike Trust came into being and, with 62 miles of road, became almost the longest of any Wiltshire trust. It controlled what became the A303 road from Mullens Pond near Thruxton to Willoughby Hedge above Mere, as well as the road from Stonehenge to Shrewton, Chitterne and Heytesbury, and several shorter sections in the vicinities of Thruxton, Amesbury and Wylye. The purpose of turnpiking local Amesbury roads - Countess Road to the parish boundary, the road from Beacon Hill to Bulford and Larkhill, and from Amesbury to Fittleton via Bulford - seems to have been to prevent travellers from by-passing Amesbury and evading the toll. Tollhouses were set up in Amesbury at the bottom of Stonehenge Road and in Countess Road (surviving), and at Bulford, as well as further afield. Milestones, of which many survive, were set up along the main roads.

The impetus for establishing the trust was provided by the 3rd Duke of Queensberry. He became the principal creditor and therefore exercised a controlling interest over its affairs. He also built Queensberry Bridge (in 1775) at his own expense. It was he of course who, as principal owner and landlord, stood to gain most from the trust's success.

The 4th Duke inherited the estate, together with the trust's debt to his predecessor of £13,060, in 1778. Over the next 30 years he urged every form of parsimony he could devise on the trust in unsuccessful attempts to recover the money. The trust made a small annual profit, but it was usually insufficient to pay even a modest interest on the Duke's loan, and certainly not enough to reduce the principal.

The first stagecoach used the turnpike for a short period in 1804, and it was greeted with such enthusiasm that some tollgates were farmed (the right to collect tolls was auctioned on an annual basis from 1792) at 50% above the normal figure. The optimism was premature, however, since most Exeter coaches continued to prefer Salisbury until the coaching zenith of the 1830s, when the increase in business, better roads and better coach design made the direct route through Amesbury practicable.

Positive steps to encourage coach traffic were made by the trustees in 1826/7, by widening the road next to the churchyard, and in 1834/5, when they purchased and demolished a house at the bottom of London Road in order to straighten the road. For no more than a decade Amesbury became an important and prosperous coaching town, with nine coaches passing through daily. Most arrived in the middle of the night and all but one used the New Inn (this is not the present New Inn but Comilla House and the adjoining building). The Exeter coaches - the Defiance, the Subscription, the Telegraph, and the Devonport Mail - all traversed what became the A303, but the Swiftsure, between London and Bridgwater, passed through Chitterne.

Amesbury's success in attracting coaches away from Salisbury was spectacular while it lasted. Success encouraged new turnpikes, and two of the last roads in Wiltshire to be turnpiked were those between Old Sarum and Amesbury (1836), and between Amesbury, Rushall and East Kennett (1840). These were not part of the Amesbury Turnpike Trust, but came under the jurisdiction, respectively, of the Swindon, Marlborough and Everleigh Trust, and the Kennet and Amesbury Trust. Too late to profit from the coaching bonanza they have nevertheless left their mark on more recent road development, since the present A345 follows their alignment on most of its course between Salisbury and Rushall.

By 1842 railways had reached Bath and Southampton and the coaching era had died almost overnight. The few coaches which struggled on were only interested now in providing feeder services between important towns, such as Devizes and Salisbury, and the nearest railway station. Amesbury and the A303 were forgotten; the Amesbury Trust's income dropped from £1,181 in 1839 to £370 in 1845. This was not the end of the Amesbury Trust, however; business continued until 1868, when a bondholder took possession of the gates; and in 1871 the trust, in common with many others, was wound up by Act of Parliament. Responsibility for roads passed to the newly established Amesbury Highway Board and an auction was held at the George Inn, Amesbury, to sell the trust's tollhouses, gates and effects. It is hard, now that the A303 has become one of the busiest roads in southern England, to realise that for some eighty years, from the demise of the stagecoaches in the 1840s until the growth of motoring in the 1920s, the main road through Amesbury was practically deserted by long-distance traffic. Thomas Hardy, writing in 1895 of events some years earlier, remarked on "the desolation which had come over this once lively thoroughfare", and Ella Noyes in 1913 commented that: One rarely sees any object moving on these roads. A waggon, growing from little to large as it slowly approaches; a solitary wayfarer on foot or bicycle; a meteoric motor car swallowed up as soon as it is seen.[74]

Shopkeepers and Tradesmen

The volume of traffic generated by small, inaccessible and largely self-sufficient communities was not great, and it was found to be most convenient to conduct one's business at the weekly market in the local town.[75] Until the lines of communication were improved and the principle of mass production introduced in the 18th century, market trading was the basis of economic life for both the market town and its hinterland. Markets had been held at Amesbury since the 13th century (as we have seen), but by 1750 the concept of a market was beginning to lose its appeal. The great fire of 1751 probably hastened its demise and by 1809 the market house was considered redundant and demolished. The broad market place, now Salisbury Street, and the weighing engine have vanished along with the market house, although the lock-up, the symbol of pie-powder (marketing) justice, remains in the guise of an estate agent's and insurance office. By 1830, according to the directory of that year, Amesbury market had become merely nominal.

The fairs, by contrast, of which Amesbury boasted four, lasted longer. These annual events were important to the agricultural community for the large-scale exchange of livestock and produce which took place, and for hiring labour. Their dates, 17th May, 22nd June, 6th October and the first Wednesday after 16th December, were of great antiquity, associated with the feast days of St Melor and the summer and winter solstices. The May and December fairs seem to have taken place in the town itself, the latter, known as the Amesbury short fair, being the more important in the early 19th century, as William Kemm recalled: "I have seen when I was very young [ie. ca.1820] the Back Lane [School Lane], the turning to Bakehouse Lane [Earls Court Road], and some way along Bakehouse Lane, full of horses at these fairs." The October fair, known as Countess Court Fair, was traditionally held on the downs above Countess, and the June fair was traditionally associated with Stonehenge.[76] The insidious changes of the 18th and 19th centuries, however, sounded the death knell for the fairs as well as the market, and Amesbury, like the majority of Wiltshire towns, became a place of shopkeepers.

A last echo of Amesbury's traditional market for local produce. A quiet moment for Harold Simmance, one of the last small-holders in Holders Road, at his stall in the 1950's.

Early directories provide abundant evidence of the shopping habits of our Victorian predecessors. At first, doubtless as a legacy of the market, Amesbury contained a number of quite specialised tradesmen: a soap-boiler, brandy merchant, peruke- [wig] maker and sieve-maker (1793); a slop- [cheap clothing] seller, two straw-bonnet makers and a brickmaker (1839). These rubbed shoulders with more predictable tradesmen, who occur consistently throughout the 19th century and later: innkeepers, bakers, grocers, drapers, blacksmiths, a saddler, wheelwright and hairdresser, amongst many others. Other trades appear to have declined in importance towards the end of the century, whether because of changing social habits or different channels of supply. No maltsters occur after 1875, although there were two until that year; similarly the trade of beer retailer (permitted under the 1830 Beerhouse Act), which reached its zenith with four traders so described in 1865, had fallen to one by 1885. In the matter of clothing no milliners appear after 1842, the three tailors of 1793 have become two in 1839 and one in 1885, and the four boot and shoe makers who occur regularly from 1793 to 1865 fall to two thereafter. From 1885 there is only one miller instead of two.

Their places were taken by a number of new trades (or old trades under new names) and an increasing number of services. A cattle dealer and a bookseller arrive in 1875, along with the proprietress of a fancy repository [gift shop]. In 1880 a lodging-house keeper occurs and in 1885 a music teacher and a post office. They are joined a decade later by a temperance house proprietor, a district nurse and three laundresses. And once the army was established around Amesbury a plethora of shops and services appear. The 1911 directory includes a cycle dealer, a solicitor, a coach builder, a bank, tea rooms, an estate agent and a fried fish dealer. Amesbury had arrived in the 20th century.

Too much reliance should not be placed on directory entries, since errors can be detected and quality and thoroughness fluctuate. Taken overall, however, they present a coherent picture of a small rural town in the 19th century, adjusting at first to the loss of its market, and then seeing its demand dwindle as the roads to Salisbury and Andover seemed ever more attractive. The coming of the army at the turn of the century provided Amesbury with a much-needed filip, but it seems that the draw of the large shopping centres has once again proved irresistible, and that in this, as in so many other respects, Amesbury has lost much of its former importance.

Chapter 6

Social Change (1539-1914)

Poverty

Between 1601 and 1834 a parish overseer of the poor existed at Amesbury (as everywhere else) whose function was to levy a rate upon the wage-earning parishioners and use the money thus raised to assist sick and invalid paupers, poor children and the elderly. An important effect of 18th century enclosure and more efficient farming methods was to increase the number of farm labourers for whom there was no work and for whose welfare the parish was responsible. As a small community with limited resources and no endowed almshouses or poorhouse, the problem of poor relief in Amesbury had become critical by the end of the 18th century. In 1792 the farmers of Amesbury petitioned their landlord, the 4th Duke of Queensberry, for the use of a former inn, the Chopping-Knife, as a poorhouse, with the following explanation:

> The poor of Amesbury are become so very poor and indolent and consequently so burthensome that the farmers are desirous to establish a poorhouse, as by that means, they apprehend, they shall be capable of keeping the real poor more conformable than they now live and oblige the indolent to work and be able to breed up the child in the habit of honesty and industry...[77]

Their appeal seems to have fallen on deaf ears, as no more is heard of the proposal, and shortly afterwards a system of supplementing the abominably low wages of farm labourers was adopted and remained until the Poor Law Amendment Act of 1834. Cobbett, in 1821, was appalled by the ragged appearance of the Wiltshire peasantry, whose discontent, in Amesbury and elsewhere, manifested itself in riots and incendiary attacks upon farm buildings in 1830.

As a result of the reforms of 1834 Amesbury became the centre of a union of 23 neighbouring parishes, which pooled their poor rate resources to build and maintain a workhouse on South Mill Hill in Amesbury.[78] Completed in 1837 it could cater for 150 inmates, with dormitories, sick wards, wash-houses, a school, chapel, boardroom, hospital and four yards. Of the 26 Wiltshire poor law unions Amesbury was the largest in terms of the area served, and yet the smallest in terms of population. In 1841 there were 106 persons resident in the workhouse, but ten years later this had dropped to 83.

Workhouses were intended to be austere, a deterrent to the idle poor.

The former workhouse in the 1930's, on the site of Avonstoke Close. Note the well-kept garden in the front and the neatly clipped hedge along the road boundary.

Amesbury workhouse was an unpleasant place, damp and dirty, with inadequate food, clothing and supervision. Whether it was worse than those of the neighbouring unions may be disputed. The scandal of the Andover workhouse is well known, and the Amesbury guardians, who administered the workhouse, whilst admitting that the diet was poor (per week there were three dinners of pea-soup, two of suet-pudding and two of three ounces of cooked bacon), made the point that it was better than the standard of living of labourers in the neighbourhood.

The guardians did come in for official criticism, however, which was met by the provision of extra wards in 1873. Thereafter conditions seem gradually to have improved. The workhouse continued in operation until 1930, when it became a Public Assistance Institution under the control of Wiltshire County Council. It was demolished in 1966/7.

Fires

The most sudden and catastrophic event in the life of any town was a major fire. Combustible building materials and inadequate firefighting equipment, coupled with the widespread use of open fires for many industrial and household processes, spelled disaster for many communities. In Amesbury nine major fires are recorded between 1700 and 1914, the most serious of which, in June 1751, devastated the High Street, causing £10,000 damage and destroying 33 houses.[79] For several of the victims this was the second time that their businesses had been reduced to ashes, for a smaller fire had struck the same area six years earlier, claiming one fatality and the lives of a number of horses.[80] Other serious fires occurred in the High Street-Salisbury Street area in 1803, when at least seven houses and other buildings were destroyed,[81] and again in 1899, when the Wesleyan Chapel and temperance hotel were lost.[82]

Amesbury's firemen pause to survey the results of the devastating Ivydene fire of 1911. With the ineffectual equipment of the time, their efforts would have been directed more at containment.

The humbler dwellings of Coldharbour and Bakehouse Lane (Earls Court Road) were no less vulnerable. Two cottages in Coldharbour were destroyed by fire in 1848[83] and a conflagration in 1899 claimed a row of thatched cottages opposite Earls Court Farmhouse[82] - a drunken navvy employed on building the branch railway line was held responsible for this blaze. A further six buildings in Smithfield Street, including the post office and Ivydene Hotel were burnt down in 1911, an event still deeply implanted on the memories of one or two of the oldest residents.[84]

In the event of a fire it was in everyone's interest to try at all costs to stop it spreading. Amesbury was perhaps luckier than other towns in having had, in the 17th century, a vicar, Thomas Holland, who made his name as an inventor of hydraulic engines and pumps.[85] An 'apparatus for extinguishing fires' which he had devised still existed in the church at the time of the mid-19th century alterations; in 1771 it may have been housed in a building in Tanners Lane (Flower Lane) described as 'The Engine House'. The two major fires of 1899,

43

however, found Amesbury unprepared to fight them. In the absence of a local brigade the teams from Salisbury and Netheravon arrived too late to prevent the fires gaining a complete hold. Indeed, in the case of the Bakehouse Lane fire, the alarm was raised by a cyclist who rode to Salisbury at 2 am; it was 5 am before the brigade was on the scene. The disaster led, by 1902, to the establishment of an Amesbury Fire Brigade,[86] which in 1911, although unsuccessful in saving the building, was able to respond to the Ivydene fire, "with alacrity."

The devastation caused by fire cannot be overestimated. Some victims were insured, it is true, and it comes as no surprise to find the postmaster in early directories doubling as insurance agent, but for those without insurance the events of an evening could result in a humiliating appeal to charity or a visit to the workhouse.

Religion

We have already hinted that the dissolution of Amesbury Priory was an act of secular, rather than spiritual, importance to the town. Responsibility for the parish church passed from the prioress to the Dean and Canons of Windsor, but little is known about the impact of the reformation on the spiritual life of Amesbury, although a mood of apathy and submission prevailed in Wiltshire generally. Certainly no incumbent of the town risked his neck by opposition to whichever creed was imposed upon him. It is tempting to surmise from the surviving records that the established church in Amesbury, as elsewhere, has never since the reformation attracted any great enthusiasm in the breasts of the parishioners. In 1662, for instance, the forlorn churchwardens reported to the bishop that the church and chancel, as well as some seats in the church, "are something out of repair," and further:

> There are many that absent themselves from sermons. There are many that refuse to have their children baptized, or themselves to receive the communion. There are many that refuse to come to church to give thanks to God for their safe deliverance. There are many that refuse to pay their duty for Easter offerings to our minister.[87]

A century later the position seems to have been much the same. The vicar in 1783 replied to questions from his bishop that, "four or five and twenty is the usual number [of communicants]"[88] - the population of the parish was then probably 600-700. In Victorian Amesbury, however, when churchgoing was more commonplace, the number of communicants was about 70 in 1864,[89] and the congregation much larger, and increasing. The vicar could nevertheless report in 1870:

> Great indifference to religious duties in some of the higher class, and great immorality in the lower. But I do not know that these such impediments exist here to a greater extent than in other parishes severally.[90]

Two incumbents of Amesbury deserve mention. Thomas Holland, vicar after the commonwealth, was described by a contemporary engineer as a genius, on account of his inventions.[91] Apart from designing a pump which operated the fountain of Wilton House, he installed an engine to supply water to the hill-top town of Shaftesbury. We have already mentioned the fire engine which he designed for his parishioners. Fulwar W Fowle, by contrast, was one of those 19th century churchmen whose life work was spent ministering to a single parish. When he died in 1876 he had been vicar of Amesbury for 59 years (longer than anyone else), and had, as he himself pointed out in a sermon a few years before his death, conducted more burials than the entire population of the parish when he arrived.[92] During his incumbency he was involved in many of the developments which took place in the town in the 19th century, as well as presiding over the restoration of the church and considerable improvements to his vicarage. It is sad that the memorial to him which used to be on the south wall of the nave was removed some years ago, and is believed now to be in store in a coal shed.

Besides apathy the established church had to contend with dissent. One of the earliest and most vigorous nonconformist congregations in Wiltshire was active in the Amesbury area before the Toleration Act of 1689. Its leading light was John Rede, a magistrate of the Anabaptist persuasion, who lived at Birdlimes Farm, Porton.[93] His inaugural meeting in 1655 attracted over 100 sympathisers from the surrounding villages, and soon meetings were being held in various places, including the house of Thomas Long at West Amesbury, which in 1669 attracted a congregation of about 30, and was still active in 1683.[94] The initial enthusiasm seems to have died with the Toleration Act, since no dissenting congregation is listed in an early-18th century survey, and only one building was registered for protestant dissenters' worship at that time (the house of Thomas Cook in 1719).[95]

Dissent returned to Amesbury in the person of John Wesley, who visited the town twice, in 1779 and 1785. After the latter visit he noted in his journal: "I visited the little flock at Amesbury, humble, simple, and much devoted to God."[96] Wesley made a profound impression on the town, reawakening an interest in religion, which resulted in a number of Independent [Congregationalists], and later Methodist, meetings springing up in private houses in Amesbury, Ratfyn and West Amesbury.[97] Even a barn was used. The first mention of a Methodist chapel occurs in 1816, and this was relicensed in 1838. It is probably the one which stood on a site behind the present chapel in High Street, which was destroyed by fire in 1899. Writing with disdain of this congregation in 1867, Fulwar Fowle commented, "among the lower orders, many who are not dissenters, go with itching ears to hear the sermon."[98] After the disaster of 1899 the community rallied to such an extent that the present building was completed and opened within 12 months of the fire.

Until recently Catholicism seems to have played no part in the post-reformation history of Amesbury. The only exception occurred between 1794 and 1800, when (as we have seen) the abbey mansion was rented to refugee canonesses from Louvain. They deserve mention, if only for the death of Sister Monica, one of their number, which occurred while they were celebrating mass on St Monica's day, 1797.

Education

Few ordinary children before the 19th century were given any formal education. The lucky ones owed what schooling they received to charitable foundations set up to employ a schoolmaster or mistress from the proceeds of the deceased benefactor's estate. John Rose (allegedly the first man to grow a pineapple in England)[99] in 1677, and Henry Spratt, in 1708, established schools in Amesbury in this fashion, the former for 20 children aged 9-15, the latter for 30 children aged 4-9.[100] Rose's school was originally held in the south transept of the parish church, possibly succeeding an earlier school in the same place; in 1807, after many years of teaching in the schoolmaster's house, it was transferred to the former Jockey Inn in High Street, known to this day as the Old Grammar School. One of its earliest and most distinguished pupils may have been Joseph Addison, born at nearby Milston. Spratt's School never owned premises, the teaching being carried on in the schoolmistress's house. Reading and the catechism were the pupil's first concerns, and until these were mastered they could not pass from Spratt's to Rose's school, where they would learn English grammar, arithmetic, fair writing, cyphering and casting of accounts.

In the 19th century the range of education available to Amesbury children was greatly expanded. The two charity schools continued throughout the century, and the trustees of Rose's charity, having accrued a surplus, began a preparatory school in 1819, which continued, under the direction of the Misses Sandell in their own house until the 1840s. From 1821 until its demise in 1896 Spratt's school was run by female members of the Zillwood (or Selwood) family, while Rose's school plodded on under the tuition of two notable masters, William Cox, 1801-49, and Edward Flower, 1871-99. A host of new schools also sprang up. A Lancasterian school (based on the monitoring theories of the educationalist Joseph Lancaster) had been established by 1830 and this became, by 1839, the National School, the largest school in Victorian Amesbury, providing an elementary education to as many as 100 pupils. This school was managed by the Antrobus family in premises of their own, and by 1855 they had augmented it by the provision of an infants' school. This continued under a succession of spinster mistresses until the turn of the century. Besides these more or less permanent institutions, and a school held at the workhouse, a succession of temporary schoolteachers pass through the directories catering for the higher social strata: Miss Caroline Browne, whose day-school (1842) became a boarding school (1855-65) and who died at an advanced age in 1881; Mr John Zillwood, related to the mistresses of Spratt's school, who ran a day school between 1855 and 1875; and the Rev Arthur Meyrick, who operated "a preparatory school for young gentlemen" at Wyndersham House [Fairholme] from 1875 to 1880. Taking all these establishments together it seems likely that in mid-Victorian Amesbury upwards of 200 children were receiving schooling in Amesbury, and this figure, estimated from directories, tallies extremely well with the 1851 census returns discussed in chapter four.

Besides the schooling of young children two opportunities existed for older pupils. A charity established in 1725 by Richard Harrison offered apprenticeships for up to five former pupils of the charity schools. By the end of the 19th century awards under this bequest had become sporadic, and the last apprenticeship was awarded in 1897. Rather more successful was an adult evening school, begun in 1859 and conducted by Mr Merchant, the postmaster, at the Wesleyan chapel, which continued with enthusiasm and a government grant until at least 1870.

Towards the end of the Victorian era state supervision of education increased. A School Attendance Committee for the Amesbury Union was established in the 1880s with two attendance officers. By 1900 both Rose's and Spratt's school buildings were considered defective and the National School premises had been condemned by the Education Department as unsatisfactory. Spratt's was in any case moribund and the headmaster of Rose's, Edward Flower, had intimated his wish to retire (in 1911 he is described as a bee-keeper). Negotiations took place in 1900 between Sir Edmund Antrobus, Wiltshire County Council and the trustees of the various charities with the result that, on land in Back Lane [School Lane] presented by Sir Edmund, a new school was erected at a cost of nearly £4,000, which sum was raised from the proceeds of selling the property of Rose's and Spratt's charities. Harrison's apprenticing charity was also included in the scheme, the produce of its assets being used to provide scholarships to the school. The school provided places for 137 boys and girls and 58 infants, slightly fewer than our estimate of the total attendance of the various schools some 30 years earlier.

A contingent from one of Amesbury's smaller schools in 1928, run by Mrs Cockle (centre). It's interesting to note that the larger boys seem to have manoeuvred themselves under the shade!

Into the Twentieth Century

In the course of 5,000 years Amesbury has undergone long periods of relative stability punctuated by occasional upheavals. The founding of the first abbey and the dissolution of the second were two such upheavals, events which lifted Amesbury out of its doldrums and pointed it in a new direction. A third was the agricultural revolution of the mid-18th century. The fourth, and most recent, occurred during the years 1895-1902, and marks a convenient place for this historical essay to end.

The history of Amesbury in the 20th century is best illustrated by describing what survives today, and this the second part of our book sets out to do. The seeds of Amesbury's latest revolution were sown in 1872, in which year large scale army manoeuvres took place on Salisbury Plain, centred on Beacon Hill and the site of Bulford Camp.[101] Ten years later the plain came under attack from a different direction, the business interest of the London and South Western Railway, who proposed a railway line from Grateley via Amesbury and Shrewton to Westbury.[102] A lull followed, until in 1897 both camps made a move. The army, for its part, purchased 750 acres in Bulford parish; the railway tycoons proposed to build a line up the Avon valley from Salisbury via Amesbury and Stonehenge to Pewsey. These two interests conflicted, because the railway would have made a nonsense of the army's plans to use the Avon as a practice area for river-crossings under enemy attack. The army won, the railway scheme was dropped, and a total of 42,000 acres of Salisbury Plain were, by 1902, in the ownership of the War Department. Meanwhile an enormous show of military strength had taken place on Boscombe Down, in the form of a grand review of 50,000 troops attended by 80,000 spectators. As army camps sprang up on the downs all around Amesbury it became clear that the town would take on a new role, providing services and communications to the transient hordes of soldiers and their families. It was clear, too, that to fulfil this function, Amesbury must become more accessible to the outside world. Hence the railway reappeared. On 2nd June 1902 the first train arrived at Amesbury along a new line from Grateley and Newton Toney. The line was later extended to Bulford Camp, and branches were made to serve Larkhill, Rollestone, Stonehenge and Lake Down [Druid's Lodge] Camps.

The railway has gone now, its function usurped by road transport. But communications, along with the ever-present defence establishments, are still the mainstay of Amesbury's economy. We have come a long way from the builders of Stonehenge, the royal nuns, the peasant farmers and the workhouse. The present is ephemeral. Our future will be the better for the interest we take in our colleagues, those generations of men and women who have watched the Avon wind its course timelessly through our little town.

AMESBURY: A TWENTIETH CENTURY SURVEY

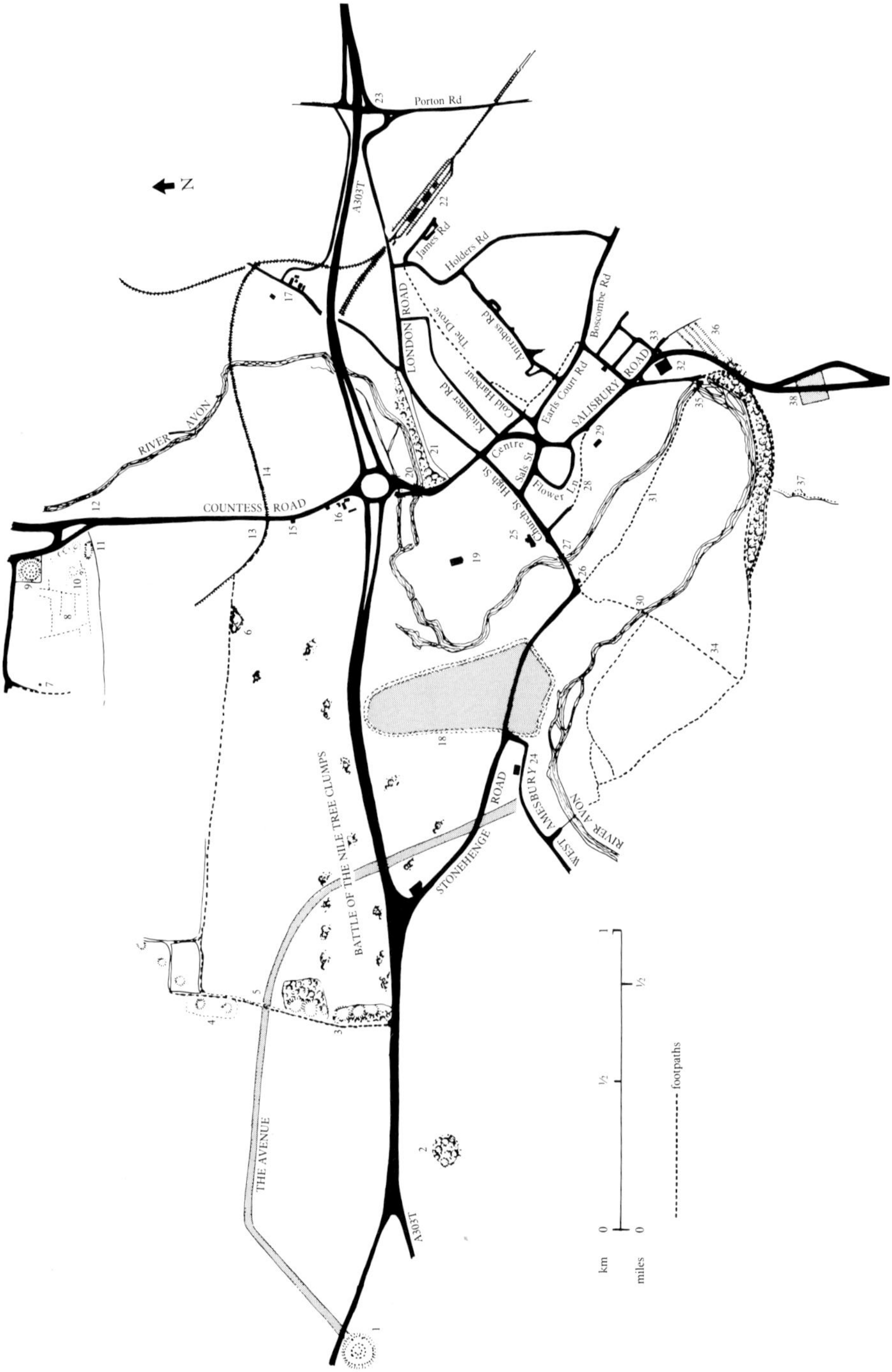
N
Porton Rd
A303T
James Rd
Holders Rd
Boscombe Rd
Antrobus Rd
The Drove
LONDON ROAD
Cold Harbour
Kitchener Rd
Earls Court Rd
SALISBURY ROAD
Centre
Sals St
Flower Ln
Church St
High St
RIVER AVON
COUNTESS ROAD
BATTLE OF THE NILE TREE CLUMPS
STONEHENGE ROAD
WEST AMESBURY
RIVER AVON
THE AVENUE
A303T
km 0 ½ 1
miles 0 ½
footpaths

Chapter 7

Introduction

The town today still sits quietly and largely out of sight in the Avon valley, waiting patiently for the passing traveller. Fortunately nowadays superior sign-posting points the way and our traveller, unlike yesteryear, does not have to wander across a hostile plain, at risk from robbers, cut-throats and rutted trackways. Development boundaries are continually being pushed way beyond those of the original groups of dwellings built to serve the needs of miller, farmer, church and lord, and have crept up the slopes surrounding the town to the high ground beyond.

The approach roads are lined with an ever-thickening ribbon of houses, primarily private developments, and large housing estates are also becoming an established part of the scene. Local authority housing is established in a solid

A GENERAL MAP OF AMESBURY

A general map of the town area showing features referred to in the text.
- - - - - - - - - - footpaths

1 Stonehenge
2 Full Moon Clump
3 New King Barrows
4 Old King Barrows
5 Seven Barrows area
6 Half Moon Clump
7 The Cuckoo Stone
8 Crop markings of early farm settlement
9 Woodhenge
10 Crop markings
11 Long barrow
12 Totterdown
13 Route of former railway, now public path
14 Route of former railway
15 Toll-house
16 Countess Farm
17 Ratfyn Farm
18 Vespasian's Camp
19 The Abbey Mansion
20 Graybridge
21 Lords Walk
22 Former railway station
23 Folly Bottom
24 West Amesbury House
25 Parish Church of St Mary & St Melor
26 Site of former toll-house
27 Queensberry Bridge (otherwise Great Bridge)
28 Almanaze Path
29 Viney's Farm House
30 Ham Hatches
31 Wittenham Footpath
32 Site of former workhouse
33 Toll-house
34 The Durnford Path
35 South Mill
36 The Lynchets
37 Ditch and Pit Alignment
38 Enclosure

quadrant from north-east around to south-east. Such industry that is permitted highlights the eastern approach, while the farming widely practised here has largely maintained a green belt to the north, west and south.

With the exception of the adjacent Boscombe Down airfield and its complex of hangars, buildings and houses positioned to meet the urgent demands of war and aircraft rather than the desires of the environmentalist, development around Amesbury has so far been managed with minimal intrusion into the countryside. There are signs that this policy which has so far been pursued relatively successfully, if unconsciously, is in the process of change and that Amesbury, even now, is evolving into yet another urban sprawl across the downland. The traditional approach has not been without its problems though, having produced some fairly high density housing estates within the natural confines, with the result that the town today is but a pale shadow of its former self.

The centre of Amesbury lies approximately in the middle of its parish. The approach is made through a landscape of field boundaries that still reflects the reorganisation brought about by enclosure during the 18th century. This pattern is itself disappearing, as the demand for more spacious fields is met in the quest for ever increasing efficiency in farming.

The parish boundary coincides fairly well with such evidence of the earlier manorial boundaries that exists, allowing for the areas that have, more recently, been added or subtracted. Perhaps this similarity gives a strong hint of common origin. Evidence of the manorial boundary is scarce. That which remains results largely from the use of man-made and topographical features. An early road marking the division between adjoining manors became the later London Road, or A303, to the east of the town; the river, from the Woodhenge area downstream to Ratfyn and similarly upstream from Normanton through West Amesbury; the line between the various tumuli on the surrounding downland and the route followed by the various streets in the town. All these features were used, as we see in an extract from the 1639 perambulation of the Earldom manor:

> ....turning south east between the said Earl's Fields and Ratfield Down to a ball or bound standing upon the top of a great Ditch....as the said ditch leadeth by - one ball between Porton Down on the S.E. and the said Hogg fflock down to the next bound....N.E. up the river to West Amesbury and so to the several fishing of Sir Lawrence Washington lately called Mr Dawbney's mill-pond....from the said ash down to the middle of the river and so taking in King's Island which is within this boundary and thence down by the same river of Avon to a stone which lieth in the middle of the river..

The remains of an early ditch and field bank feature, often used from Saxon times to mark boundaries, is visible on the downs to the south of the town, crossing the now metalled track to Durnford. Even this rare feature, though scheduled as an ancient monument has, with others, suffered the onslaught of the plough. So is our history lost. Unfortunately the assumed economics of modern farming, even when properly carried out, do not leave much time for the niceties of history. The subject rarely attracts the sympathy of the average farmer.

An earlier archaeological feature, a pit alignment and ditch rare to this region, is also thought to delineate a territorial boundary and runs in a north-south direction to the west of South Mill Hill. It had disappeared without trace until

One of the many previously unknown archaeological features that came to light during the 1976 drought was this rare pit alignment and ditch. Running southwards from South Mill Woods, it is thought to represent various phases in a territorial boundary of the iron age period, and is probably associated with the extensive settlement known to have existed in this area.

Improvements to the A345 at South Mill Hill to the south of Amesbury neatly bisected this pre-medieval enclosure, or penning, that remained undiscovered during the roadworks.

For many years associated with Stonehenge, the normally invisible 'avenue' of twin parallel banks to the north-west of the town can clearly be seen here running through the Battle of the Nile tree clumps as it turns south-west towards West Amesbury. The tree clumps have deteriorated significantly in the last ten years, through disease and age.

At the north entrance to the town, in the field adjoining the south edge of Woodhenge, the 1976 drought conditions exposed evidence of this farm settlement from the bronze age period. In the background is a barrow alignment.

1976 when the unusually dry summer caused it to show as a crop mark. Other settlement and farming features of the Romano-British period were also brought to light in the same area and to the west and north of the town.

As we have seen earlier, the approaches to Amesbury have evolved around the cardinal points through the existence of the ancient east-west trade route and the north-south river valley route which, at their intersection, provide an ideal and sheltered site for the town in the flat and fertile river plain. In earlier years our weary traveller, finding Salisbury Plain not the most hospitable of places, must have searched eagerly for signs of the town before proceeding into the depths of uncharted England.

The evolution of the road system to today's standard has, of course, been a long and far from steady process. Routes were determined largely by the local topography and seasons, giving us highways over firmer ground for the winter, and summer ways following the flatter river courses. They depended largely on whether the ground was passable, and would meander and vary as hooves and wheels made a particular portion too deeply rutted and impassable. The deep grooving that often resulted can still just be seen to the east of Amesbury where the road swings over Beacon Hill, before dropping down to Folly Bottom, and as field markings to the west just before Stonehenge. Similarly, about ten years ago, excavations to the south of the town revealed medieval wheel tracks well away from the nearest present trackway. As agricultural requirements increased, bringing the larger and more well defined field systems, the meandering routes became more and more contained within the narrow confines characteristic of today's road system, bringing of course the inevitable need for improved surfacing. We enter Amesbury today along the results of this almost timeless evolutionary process.

"Spot of trouble with the road Guv?" Pot-holes or a re-surfacing job during the 1920's would bring out this team of stalwarts, to keep the roads in repair.

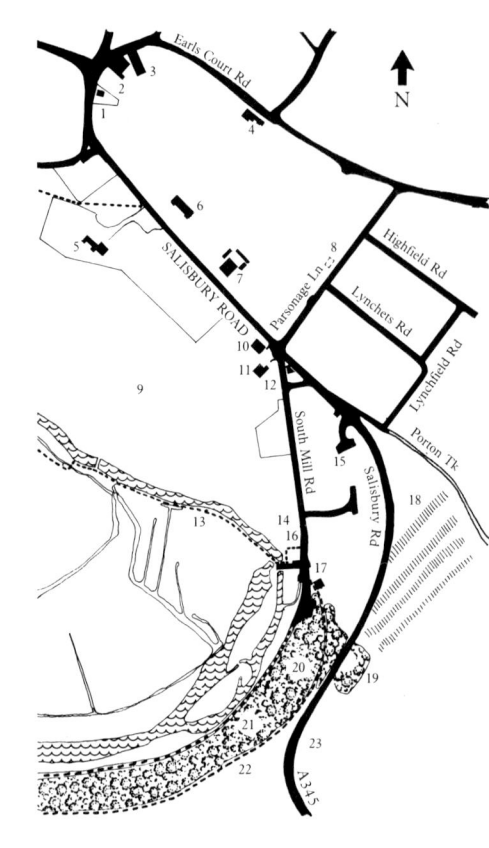

1 The Pound
2 Former Co-operative store and earlier site of Ivydene
3 Cinema
4 Earls Court Farm House
5 Vineys Farm House
6 Antrobus House
7 Red House
8 Site of former Parsonage Barn
9 Water meadows
10 Police Station
11 Buckland Court
12 Toll-house
13 Wittenham Path
14 South Mill Green
15 Avonstoke Close. Site of former workhouse
16 South Mill
17 South Mill Cottage
18 Lynchets
19 Chalk Pit
20 South Mill Wood
21 Durnford track, former Wood-way
22 Durnford track
23 South Mill Hill, formerly Lime Kiln Hill and Workhouse Hill

Chapter 8

The Approaches to the Town

South

Approaching Amesbury from the south, the traveller can take either of two classified roads. The more picturesque uses the river valley from Salisbury through the Woodfords, Lake and Wilsford, entering the town via West Amesbury. The direct and shortest road from Salisbury however, is by the A345, a route that gives a better idea of how the land rises as Salisbury Plain is reached. The line of this road dates from 1836. Prior to this travellers from the south would have come via the old Roman road, later the Marlborough Coach Road, branching northwards to Amesbury at the five mile post which is the Winterbourne Gunner turning today.

South Mill Hill Before 1836 the road from the south entered the town at Lime Kiln Hill, which was also the junction with the Durnford and West Amesbury trackways. From this point the road descended steeply towards Townsend Mill, our present South Mill. Although very overgrown the old route is still visible today and is used as a public right of way, with the bank and hedge - laid for years in the traditional manner - just discernible. The present road that curves around

At Southmill the former road from Salisbury winds its way down the hill past the house, to meet with the Durnford track on the way to Amesbury.

The 19th century toll-house at the top of Southmill Road was designed to serve traffic on the old road to the right and the new turnpike at the left. The horizon behind is now lined with houses of the Red House Farm development.

by the Lynchets was not constructed until the turnpike came into existence, the new route taking it to the east of the workhouse, part of which protruded into the road causing not a little worry to the Board of Guardians, which decided not to consult the turnpike commissioners on the matter lest they were forced to demolish the offending buildings. As inspection will reveal, it is the north-eastern corner of the old tollhouse that now catches the heavy lorry.

Returning to the earlier road at South Mill, the first habitation that the weary 18th-century traveller would meet was the cottage known today as South Mill cottage, thought to have been the 'Blue Lion' Inn. At the base of the hill, at the mill, the alternative route to Durnford and the Woodford valley joined the Salisbury road, at South Mill Green. Both merged and proceeded north-west along the present South Mill Lane which then extended into the town instead of becoming, as at present, the Salisbury Road, once past the 19th century toll house. Up to the 19th century, the road ran through the common fields, orchards and closes, a much more open environment than at present. It was, from appearance on the map, the more prosperous farming and residential part of the town. Certainly this area did not seem to possess the numbers of humble dwellings found elsewhere. The common fields immediately to the north of the mill, between South Mill Road and the river, were still used as a cricket field, fair-ground and recreation area well into the first quarter of the 20th century. It's interesting to note that the small building near the mill known in earlier years as the mortuary has now been transformed into a desirable bijou residence. Until 1967 the two principal buildings to be seen at South Mill were the mill itself and the workhouse. The mill still stands, as a private residence, but the workhouse has been replaced by Avonstoke Close, a group of town houses built on the same site. The mill and workhouse merit further consideration; particularly the latter which, although no longer with us, made such a social impact during its time.

58

The southerly approach to Amesbury viewed from South Mill Hill at the turn of the century. The workhouse is in the foreground.

A similar view in the early 1930's. Local Authority housing has appeared and already many of the once prominent trees have gone.

The present scene: the workhouse and adjacent farm buildings have gone, replaced by a residential area and police station.

The Workhouse   As we have seen elsewhere, by the 19th century a very real need existed to cater for increasing numbers of poor persons, by providing material or financial aid. Whilst the abbey existed it would have tended to the needs of the pauper element, assuming it followed normal practice, providing such clothing, food and tuition as it was able. Support of the poor later became the duty of the parish and all parishioners were returned to it if reduced to pauperism elsewhere. All this, of course, presupposes that a person was able to leave the parish or manor in the first place, for to do so a licence from the lord was required. During the Elizabethan period a poor relief system was set up which continued with varying success until the 19th century. Legislation was then introduced, resulting in the passing of the Poor Law Amendment Act in 1834.

The immediate result of the Act as far as Amesbury was concerned was for the parish to be grouped with others into the administrative unit known as the Union, and a workhouse built for the union on the southern edge of the town. The workhouse was completed and a going concern by 1838. Designed by W B Moffatt, a friend and business partner of Sir George Gilbert Scott, it took the established form of three parallel sets of buildings used as wards, dormitories, kitchens, laundries, chapel and boardroom, joined at right angles through their centre by administrative blocks with storerooms, larders, staff quarters and the "usual offices". A central tower affording a good view of the various wings and yards was also used as offices and accommodation. Pigsties, stables, mortuary and various other outhouses were situated around the periphery and a large garden was cultivated to the south. The complexities of the Victorian administrative system caused certain initial difficulties, with Returning Officers complaining that they were unable to complete the various forms and paperwork. The system of supply by competitive tendering also met with opposition from local traders who were not chosen, one in particular complaining that, "Tory tenders (were) being accepted whither cheapest, dearest, best or worst...."

Within a workhouse poor law relief was run much in accordance with the Victorian concept of making it a socially unacceptable, degrading and unattractive prospect. Men and women were segregated. Families, if admitted, were split up, perhaps not seeing each other again but certainly not being allowed to mix together. The workhouse was a thing to dread and to be avoided at all costs if possible, because once inside one rarely emerged on a permanent basis under one's own motivation! As the name of the institution implies, inmates were given work to do to retain their concept of usefulness. Men would pick oakum, grind bones for glue or tend the gardens and livestock. Women would attend to the laundry and cooking; children were given an elementary education before being sent to labour on local farms.

In return the inmates were housed and fed but enjoyed a very rudimentary existence. Their diet received continual criticism and was poor by our present standards but considered quite adequate by the Poor Law Commissioners, not so much for its nutritional value but because it was better than that which was available to the average labourer. Living conditions were poor and received their fair share of attention - the yards were muddy, the sanitation poor, with the "soil remaining in the privies..." Children, who at various times numbered up to 40, had to be of a hardy breed.

Medical assistance often left much to be desired. In January 1840 burst water pipes caused excessive dampness in the girls' bedroom. The workhouse master put a charcoal brazier in the room to dry it out, removing it 15 minutes before bedtime, and putting it downstairs. The bedroom windows were shut tight against the cold night air and the bedroom door left open. Thirty minutes later a girl entering the bedroom found the occupants being violently sick in bed. The master was called and found them "almost in a state of insensibility". He opened the windows and tried to revive the children by using a bucket of cold water. This apparently had little success so he dipped them in a bath of lukewarm water...."most providentially they all recovered". Remember, it was January and a particularly hard winter!

The workhouse master did not always appear in such a helpful or benevolent role. On one occasion he was accused of accelerating the death of a boy inmate who was ill and confined to bed. It was alleged that the boy's condition did not impress the master, who pulled him from the bed by leg and arm and threw him across the room, then picking him up and throwing him back onto the bed during which the boy hit and wounded his head on the stone wall. In the subsequent inquiry the master protested his innocence, in this case rightly, as the culprit was later found to be the schoolmaster, a man subsequently described as utterly unfit for the situation in which he was placed. This particular workhouse master was, however, later found to be guilty of beating boys with a rope's end and so he was not entirely without fault. Mind you, his youthful charges may well have driven him to desperation!

Other sad tales include allegations that an inmate with putrefying maggot-ridden wounds was allowed to lie and die of dropsy in a room occupied by healthy men and that the guardians refused to accept into the workhouse a woman "apparently in the last stage of existence." Transporting lunatics to Devizes must have been a hazardous business, with reports of the patients arriving variously with broken limbs, bound and drunk! With this sort of atmosphere prevailing it is no wonder that fighting is reported among the inmates and that escape attempts were made by whole families, whilst others preferred to take their chances in the colonies.

In spite of its shortcomings, the 19th-century poor relief system was a very important social development. Amesbury's workhouse continued to house various inmates up to the 1950's. It was also known locally as 'the Union', and as 'the Spike' from the method of filing the meal or relief tickets for the itinerant visitor who, with his distrust of authority, would hide his few belongings in a convenient hole in the bank along the Salisbury Road. It is perhaps sad to note that now the workhouse has gone, demolished in 1967, no place or road names commemorate its existence. Presumably the enlightened few who decide the content of such labels still feel a corporate guilt, generated from the currently unacceptable standards set by their forerunners. Let us quickly forget...!

South Mill   At the bottom, or southern end, of South Mill Road lies the former mill itself, the focal point of several tracks from nearby villages.

This mill is the last remaining evidence of a following practised here since before the Domesday period. The present structure is, however, a 19th century reconstruction of an older building. An earlier era is suggested by the stonework in the adjacent mill-leet just to the north, which displays more of the green sandstone from the demolished abbey. The mill was certainly working during the early 17th century, when described as containing two water-corn mills. It would have been one of two such establishments at that time, the other being situated by the present gate to the Abbey Nursing Home, next to the parish church. Milling activities had finished by the latter part of the 19th century and, during the early part of this century, the building was purchased by one "Bungy" Woods, as a dwelling and trading premises. Mr Woods, also known as "Beaver" due to his long white beard, was a master builder who came from Portsmouth. Whilst in Amesbury, he acquired possession of the common fields that lay immediately to the north-west, from the mill along the river edge to Stonehenge Road, and started a gravel pit and an ill-fated laundry along the edge of the Wittenham Path. The laundry, although built, came to naught through Mr Woods' scant regard for the planning requirements of local government. He did leave his mark, however, in the shape of the eastern-style bungalows that he built of "reinforced" concrete, in the London Road and in Church Lane. Remains of the gravel-pit workings are just visible still, with one remaining truck from the narrow-gauge railway. The foundations of the laundry can also just be depicted.

South Mill, formerly Town End Mill.

Having exhausted the potential of the area, Bungy disappeared from the scene as quickly as he had arrived. The mill however, with the arrival of electricity, embraced this new technology, using the water-power to continue the good service rendered to the community for so many years.

All that remains of Bungy Wood's once extensive gravel workings and other commercial enterprises.

Amesbury Electric Light Company   Electricity was first provided in 1922, with the formation of the Amesbury Electric Light Company which housed itself in the South Mill, purchased from Bungy Woods for around £1200. An office and showroom was set up in the High Street at Chimes House, now a hairdressers establishment, and the Company set about providing an initial supply of direct current from its Hay-Maryon water turbine generator.

The first building to reap the benefit of this modern technology was the workhouse, being directly in the path of the first line that was run to the town. At first, the capability extended only to the provision of electric light, which spread from the South Mill along Salisbury Road and Salisbury Street, branching west down Church Street, east along High Street and round to the cinema. As mentioned above, power was initially obtained from a Hay-Maryon water turbine, belt driving a Bruce-Peebles 15/17kW 220V DC dynamo, with back-up from a three-cylinder Pelapone paraffin engine - noisy, temperamental and used as little as possible. Late in 1924 a type 10H single-cylinder 70HP Ruston and Hornsby diesel, direct-coupled to a 40kW Newton dynamo was introduced.

The demand for electricity was ever increasing, necessitating the eventual provision of additional generating plant. In 1925 a second water turbine was installed, identical to the first except that it was direct-coupled to a Bruce-Peebles dynamo. The capacity of the available water power being eventually taken up, a further oil engine had to be installed in the late twenties, a 100HP three-cylinder marine type Allen diesel engine, direct-coupled to a 65kW Newton dynamo. An excerpt from the Amesbury Parish Council Guide for 1926 read "The Parish Council have considerably more then 50 street lamps lit each night and the parish is considered to be one of the best-lit places of the neighbourhood". The Managing Director and the Secretary of the Company were respectively Chairman and Secretary of the Parish Council.

The engineering staff of the Amesbury Electric Light Company in the late 1930's. From left to right: Ted Hibberd, linesman; Ernest Sparey, linesman's mate; Arthur Rolfe, electrician; Reg Denham, electrician (one of two brought in for the period of changeover from DC to AC and for updating consumers installations); Doug Smith, electrician's mate; Frank Field, engineer in charge from 1922 until final close-down; George Snook, engineer.

In 1932 the Amesbury Electric Light Company was taken over by the Mid-Southern Utilities Ltd, of Aldershot. Sometime after takeover, to augment its ever-stretched generating capabilities, the Amesbury company took a single-phase 11kW underground supply from the Wessex Electricity sub-station at Ratfyn, to a sub-station in School Lane and started the very slow process of changing over from DC to AC - a process that was later slowed, of course, by the war. By 1935 all the generators at the mill were running at full capacity, with a maximum evening load of approximately 99kW in the winter. Not another ampere of current could be produced, nor was there room to install additional equipment. The demand for electricity began to become critical, with various parts of the day having to be watched very carefully - the early morning domestic load was one in particular. Another was the dough-mixers in the bakeries in the town. As they started up, the engineers in the mill would gaze anxiously at their meters, watching the process of mixing the dough reflected in the rising pulsations of the pointers!

It was, therefore, fortuitous that eventually the Wessex Electricity Company appeared on the scene, in the form of a 33kV alternating current supply line from its station at Wilton, overland to Andover, passing close to South Mill. This line possessed sufficient spare capacity for Amesbury to benefit from a three-phase 11kV supply, and the situation was saved. In 1945 the Amesbury Electric Light Company came into the hands of the Wessex Electricity Company and, now stretched to the limit, began to run down, no longer able to meet the still rising demand for electricity. In 1948 the Wessex Electricity Company became nationalised, eventually becoming the Southern Electricity Board.

During the time it was in service, the Amesbury power station at South Mill only failed in its duties once. One night, in the late 1920's, a large elm was blown down in a gale, severing all the lines from the station, pulling the cables and their anchorage from the wall of the mill and leaving a large hole!

Salisbury Road At the top of South Mill Road, at its junction with Salisbury Road and on the site of former farm buildings, stands the modern police station erected in 1976 with the adjacent Buckland Court, a home for elderly persons. The new police station here, represents the latest stage of keeping the locals in order, although nowadays the immediate community probably represents the least problem to the Amesbury police. The building contains two items of carved stone-work removed, in spite of considerable public outcry, from the former Edwardian style police station in School Lane that it replaces. A carved crest can be seen on the outer south wall and a reproduction of Stonehenge is situated within the front entrance.

Here also is the later of Amesbury's tollhouses. This one, built in 1836, is positioned at the junction of the turnpike and the earlier road, to take tolls from those travelling on the new turnpike between Amesbury and Old Sarum.

Nearer to Amesbury is Red House, the former farm house and part of the reorganisation that appears to have evolved from the process of enclosure. The house is thought to have been rebuilt around the beginning of the 18th century, in brick with a moulded stone string-course and many other points of architectural character. Some of the interior character and fittings suggest an earlier period. It retains today only a walled garden and paddock as a reminder of the era in which it formed the focal point of a sizeable country farm. During recent work in the grounds the foundations of additional and possibly earlier premises were discovered at the rear of the main building. Considerable redevelopment is underway here; the former coach house is being converted into dwellings and a further development proposal exists for more on the corner area. To the left of Red House, approaching Amesbury, lies Antrobus House. Another red-brick building, this one was erected in 1924 as a memorial to Colonel Sir Edmund Antrobus. It fulfilled the function of meeting hall and museum, the latter containing items of local origin and also those collected by members of the Antrobus family during their various travels. The museum no longer exists but some selected paintings and items of porcelain have been retained on display. Both the ground and first-floor rooms of the house are now available with limited facilities for public functions. The Town Council meets in the upper "Lady Florence Room".

Red House, photographed here in 1915.

A 19th century view of Viney's (formerly Vinons) Farm House.

Across the road from Antrobus House is the mid-16th century Viney's Farm House, possibly the oldest house in the town. Known originally as Vinon's farm house it still bears the name of the family for so long associated with it and with the town. Reduced to the status of farm cottages during the first half of the 20th century, its present use as an art and craft centre helps to restore to it some of its former quality. This area too, is the subject of pending redevelopment with houses and flats. It is understood that as part of the agreement, the 18th century granary, a listed building, is to be refurbished and resited nearer to the fire station. The hope for conservation of the granary was first expressed in 1973; sixteen years later nothing has happened and the building is now in a pretty parlous state so hopefully its conservation will occur before it falls down!

The other trackway joining the Salisbury Road at its junction with South Mill Road brought people from Porton, as its name implied. This track leaves the Old Marlborough Road at Stockport Bottom and approaches the town in a north-westerly direction, finally dropping down over the southern scarp at the eastern edge of the Lynchets.

The Pickfords furniture depository, built during the 1920's. The garden nursery behind it has fallen prey to residential development and now the depository itself is being considered for conversion into dwellings.

Earls Court Road and Parsonage Lane The last route from the south brought people from Newton Toney, Allington and Idmiston to the weekly markets, the fairs and the festivals. These individual routes merged and eventually entered Amesbury as the 18th century Bakers, or Bakehouse, Lane which was renamed during the early part of this century to Earl's Court Road, the name being modified in the 1930's to Earl's Road and finally reverting to its present name of Earl's Court Road in 1954.

The principal building in this road, apart from the primary school of Christ the King, is the early 19th century Earls Court Farmhouse, another product of the land enclosure process. All but one of the thatched cottages which used to line this road have been demolished over the years, some being lost in the 1960's when the fish and chip shop was built, and when the road was widened earlier this century. A little of the former character of the road is still visible in the mid-19th century Yew Cottage. The last of the earlier cottages, of brick and tile construction to the right of the school entrance, was demolished in 1985 to make way for another small town house development.

Earls Court Road. Earls Court Farmhouse, the late 19th century farm overseers' dwellings beyond it, and one of the few remaining lengths of cob walling in the foreground provide a glimpse of earlier character.

In between this road and the South Mill-Salisbury Road complex lay Bartnett Field, separated from the town in the 18th century by Parsonage Lane. Still known as Parsonage Road, the full significance of the name is now lost. Until the mid 1950's, the road contained Parsonage Barn, a wood and thatched structure of 18th century character, situated opposite Highfield Road. It was demolished to make way for the playing field of Christ the King Catholic School. The barn and the road had been so named for at least 200 years. A Parsonage Close existed in Earls Court during the early 18th century.

It is possible that these sites were all that remained of the glebe land or, alternatively, may have evolved from former holdings of the monastic community. This latter possibility may be indicated by the presence of Black

Cross Field, a name associated with a religious site or holding, which joined Bartnett Field at its southern edge. However, by the mid 19th century only Parsonage Road remained of that name; the other references had gone and did not even appear in the tithe award map, suggesting that all ecclesiastical connections, if they had ever existed, had ceased by that time. Today, the northern part of Bartnett Field adjoining Parsonage Road contains a local authority housing estate dating mainly from the 1930's intersected by the linking Highfield, Lynchfield and Lynchets Roads.

North

Keeping to the north-south theme for the moment, after the early 19th century the main road to Amesbury from the north was along the Countess Road of today, following the high ground on the western side of the river. Prior to this, access would have been along what is now the Old Marlborough Road, through Bulford and Ratfyn to the town. Additional access existed as a branch from the Devizes to Salisbury road, to the west of Amesbury. Minor tracks also existed, joining the local villages and hamlets. Entering the town from this direction in the Spring presents one with the golden display from the thousands of daffodils recently planted on the central reservation of the by-pass roundabout and along the edges of the road towards the town, the planting made possible by money donated by the Amesbury Carnival Committee.

Countess Road Countess Road seems to have assumed its present importance only since the turnpike era. Its age is not certain; it may have been the 18th century Dark Lane, referred to in the manorial court records but it would appear to be of some antiquity. Dropping down from the high ground to the north of the town at the manorial boundary, it descended to the lower ground of the river valley through steep banks forming a narrow passage. Now broadened, hard surfaced and forced to conform to 20th century requirements, a glimpse of its early character can be seen at the tollhouse which was built in approximately 1762. Here, the original road level can be deduced from the drop to the doorstep. The road was widened in the 1950's, the earlier east bank at the tollhouse site being situated more or less where the present road centre lies.

The first buildings to be seen on this route into Amesbury during the 18th century would have been the tiny tollhouse with its turnpike gate and adjacent farm cottages. Today, of course, almost the entire length of the road is built up with a 20th century ribbon development which would be unpopular with present planning laws.

North of the river, the oldest buildings apart from the tollhouse are the barns and house of Countess Farm. The front portion of the house is late 18th century and is an addition to the rear half the general character of which indicates early to mid 17th century, the steeply pitched roof suggesting it was designed to take thatch.

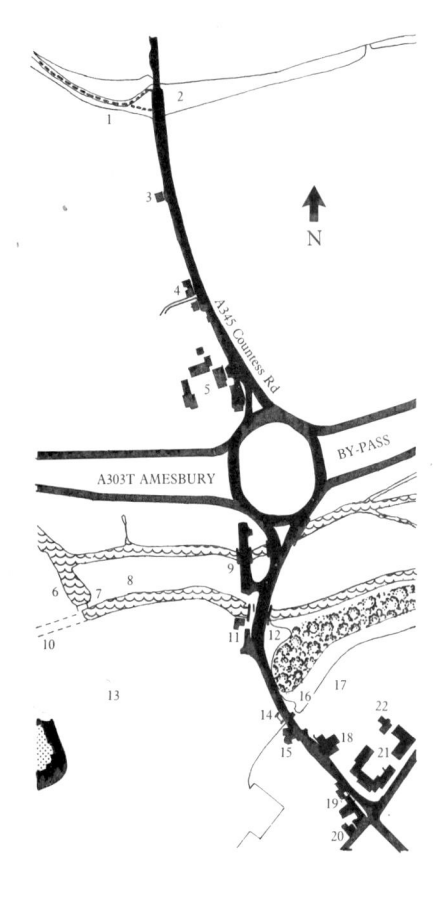

1 Former military railway, now public path to Larkhill, etc.
2 Route of former military railway
3 Toll-house
4 Farm cottages
5 Countess Farm
6 Upper Folds
7 Bowles hatches
8 Lower Folds
9 Northern Graybridge
10 Course of former canal
11 Diana House
12 Gray Bridge Hill
13 Abbey Park
14 Abbey Gates
15 Kent House
16 Lord's Walk
17 Town-End Little Field
18 Druids Restaurant
19 Comilla House and stables
20 Former bank and hardware shop
21 Countess Court and Cloisters retirement homes
22 Roman Catholic Church

The adjacent 18th century traditional barns are generally kept in good condition by caring owners. The barn to the south of the house has the year of construction 1772 inscribed by its builder, one J Osgood, thought to have been a Cholderton man.

At this point however, any original character of the road has been swept away by the modern junction roundabout with the A303. Careful afforestation carried out at the time of construction of the by-pass has helped to blend it into the surrounding countryside but, at the time of writing, the harmony of the area is being further disrupted by the construction of a motorists' service area at the north-east corner of the roundabout. The character is partially restored on the southern side of the roundabout where the former road exists now as a layby at the west side of the new road. However, in the last ten years this has become overgrown and unkempt, a parking place for heavy lorries and with a tip for hardcore close by. What character there was is diminishing visibly. Further development at the south-west corner of the roundabout is currently under way.

The 18th century toll-house in Countess Road, erected by the Amesbury Turnpike Trust.

Estate cottages and bridge in Countess Road. The cottages were demolished when the A303 Amesbury by-pass was constructed. The area is now a lay-by at the junction with the A345.

Countess Farm House and barn.

The predecessor to the stone bridge here was the "norther gray-bridge" of the 1639 perambulation where, after running north from the town along the roadway, the boundary between the Priory and Earldom Manors turned west to follow the centre of the river, passing the Upper and Lower Folds on the south bank until turning north again at Bocker Mead after two furlongs. Crossing the river and following the present road into Amesbury leads to the ascent of the scarp formed by the river meanderings. Here, on the west side, are two buildings constructed during the early 17th century, the Earl of Hertford's period of ownership, with later additions. The buildings are of similar character, showing good stonework, unusual architectural features in the form of the octagonal towers with their ogee roofs and a considerable extent of knapped flintwork ranging from superior to mediocre. The building at the bottom of the hill is inscribed and dated "Diana her Hous 1600". Kent House, at the top of the hill, is dated 1607. The precise purpose of Diana House is uncertain but various possibilities have been suggested - boating house, hunting lodge, gazebo or even the residence of some official on the estate. It appears that it may originally have stood just outside the estate wall. Its presence close to the river and to an earlier road bridge that has since been modified may be significant. The dedication of the house to the goddess of hunting may also be a key to its existence. Close by, a gateway has been introduced into the roadside wall. An attempt has been made to follow the general architectural character, but the stonework and meagre ball finials of the piers do not reflect the abilities of the earlier craftsmen.

Ascending the hill into Amesbury one reaches the second of these distinctive buildings. This one has been appreciably enlarged over the years as can be seen from the varying standards of flintwork, comparison of the present plan with that in the 18th century map and by the changes in architectural features. This was the gatehouse for the 17th century, and earlier, principal entrance to the abbey park as can be seen from the adjacent gates. The main approach to the park was from the east, along Lord's Walk, formerly Lord Carleton's Walk, after the owner who greatly influenced the layout of the grounds during the early part of the 18th century. One's presence in Lord's Walk today does not readily permit the visualisation of an impressive approach to the abbey, although the truncated remains of the twin rows of trees that flanked the former driveway do still lend a certain grandeur to the scene. Once inside the gate the vista improved, with the regimented lines of lime trees leading to the mansion but today this entrance is of minor importance and sees little use. The gatehouse here, known as Kent House, was also the farmhouse of the Park Farm.

It is just a short step now to the end of this road, at its junction with the London Road. The orchards that formerly lined the route here are gone. On the west side is the walled garden of Comilla House. Since redevelopment of the house as an elderly persons retirement home, the wall has, as predicted, been demolished and replaced with one which attempts, rather lamely, to reflect the character of its predecessor. The former stables, later a doctor's surgery and garage, shows some superior chalk block construction. It is now used as living quarters, its character marred to some extent by its ragged meeting with the new wall. Opposite this, the

Diana House and Countess Road as they appeared up to the late 1960's.

The changes brought about by the by-pass can be seen in this illustration. The quiet rural setting of Diana House has been eroded by the demands of modern road transport.

A view today of the north entrance to the town central area, with the 17th century abbey park lodge, late Park Farm House and now Kent House, at the right.

Kent House south view. When used as a lodge for the main entrance to the abbey park, principal access would have been on the north side.

74

present Druids Motel replaces the earlier Smokey Joe's and Millards Cafe of the post-war era and Colonial Restaurant of the early years of this century. A proposal exists to redevelop this site into flats. The thatched cottages at the north-east corner of the junction disappeared around 1920, leaving only Comilla House opposite, part of the former New Inn, to indicate some of the earlier character of this area. Careful study of this house shows many alterations that have taken place over the years to convert its style from country inn to well-appointed house. The last resident in Comilla House as a family home was Dr Philip Neighbour. His surgery, held in the converted stables, is now reconstructed as a display in the Salisbury and South Wiltshire Museum.

East

Prior to the 18th century a traveller approaching Amesbury from the east would come uphill from Cholderton and swing west over Haradon Hill, now Beacon Hill. He would have been presented with an open view, all traces of the town again being hidden by the river valley. The undulating scrub and grass covered Plain stretched before him with only grazing cattle, the large flocks of sheep with their attendant shepherds clad sometimes in rough white cloaks, to greet the eye.

By the 18th century agriculture had become more centralised than that of earlier periods as can be witnessed by the various groups of "Celtic" field systems still defined in the present landscape. They serve as a reminder of those times when local inhabitants were grouped into the smaller and more dispersed communities from which our present system has evolved. This east-west route, having stood the comings and goings of man since prehistoric times, must have seen many such changes in the agricultural scene as owners, fashions, methods and the levels of civilisation varied over the years.

In inclement weather, the traveller could branch right in a northerly direction instead of descending into Amesbury, and take the higher ground through Bulford and on westwards along the Packway through Shrewton. Alternatively, he could approach the town along the London Way, which corresponds to the present A303. Until Amesbury's by-pass was built in 1970 one would cross the road to Bulford at Folly Bottom before ascending the final rise into the eastern end of the town to join the London Road. Access to the town from the east today can be via three routes, of which London Road is the most direct. The other two are Kitchener Road and the Drove, both being accessible from the London Road, the latter via a footpath.

The Railway In 1902 a distraction appeared on the hitherto relatively tranquil scene in the form of the railway, of which practically all trace has now disappeared. The station lay to the south of London Road, at its east end, on the site that the Amesbury Transport Company and other local light industries occupy today. The line passed north-south under the road with the single track to

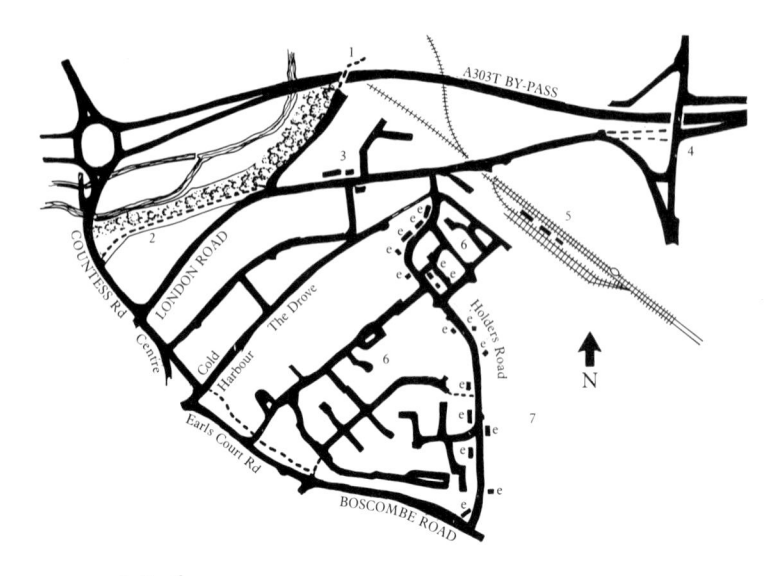

1 Ratfyn
2 Lord's Walk
3 Concrete Bungalows
4 Folly Bottom
5 Railway Station
6 Farm Holdings (Now Local Authority Housing Estate)
7 Farm Holdings
e Experimental Houses

Bulford and beyond curving eastwards on its embankment as it passed Ratfyn Farm. Provision of this amenity became feasible only after the Basingstoke to Salisbury line was authorised in 1854. Access to London and beyond then became easily available; horizons receded for trade and travel and from this began the decline of Amesbury's market and fair as they had been established for centuries. First attempts to provide rail transport were not successful. A line planned to run through Amesbury, Shrewton, Westbury and eventually reach Bristol was defeated in Parliament in 1883 by opposition from the Great Western Railway which held a virtual monopoly of traffic from London. A further proposal in 1896 for a north-south route following the Avon valley and serving Salisbury, the Woodfords, Durnford, West Amesbury, Amesbury and onwards to Durrington and eventually Pewsey met with opposition from the War Office as such a route would bisect its newly acquired training area on Salisbury Plain. Local farmers on the other hand were eager to offer land in the valley for the railway and sidings.

The line which was the outcome of all this wrangling was largely instigated by the military authorities which probably accounted for its bias towards a service from London rather than a local catchment area. Public traffic commenced in 1902, by the London and South Western Railway. Two years later the junction

These two views reflect the normal rural tranquillity of Amesbury's railway station between the wars.

As a contrast, the periods of intense activity for the station during wartime are typified here.

A special working headed by Class M7 0-4-4T No 30108 prepares to leave Amesbury on March 23rd 1963, eleven years after regular passenger services had ceased on the branch.

with the Salisbury-Basingstoke line was improved to allow easy access to Salisbury. This permitted the setting-up of a useful local service at a time when road transport was still in its infancy.

The strategic importance of the railway did not, of course, escape the notice of the Army. At the outbreak of the 1914-18 world war a further line was constructed from Amesbury to serve Larkhill, Stonehenge airfield, Rollestone balloon school and the other military establishments at that time on the Plain which had begun to feel the effects of concentrated troop training. This military line commenced at Ratfyn, crossed the river valley to Countess Road by viaduct and proceeded north-west towards Larkhill, etc. It was taken up in 1937, rail activity reverting to primarily passenger and freight services between Salisbury, Amesbury and Bulford plus the other intervening villages. Passenger traffic continued until 1952 and freight until 1963 when the line was closed as part of the economy measures.

The railway station grew very quickly from its original modest country status and was rapidly enlarged to cope with the wartime requirement, its four platforms at times being packed with military personnel. In its later years, it reverted to its rural characteristics, with only the turntable, unused marshalling tracks and extensive signalling to tell of former activities.

The railway was closed to passenger traffic in 1952 and finally closed down in 1965 when the permanent way, despite the title, was taken up. The station, bridges and buildings are gone and the Ratfyn sidings area although truncated by the A303 by-pass and rapidly filling as an industrial park, is still definable. A reminder of its presence is shown by the east wall of the former Home Farm Model Dairies, the line of which had to accommodate the boundary with the sidings. The railway staff cottages built solidly of red brick in typical style still stand at the entrance to the transport yard, outshone by the relative magnificence of the former station-master's house on the corner of London Road and Holders Road. The routes of the two railways can still be traced fairly easily, some lengths being public rights of way leading to Newton Toney.

Boscombe Down Another significant aspect of Amesbury's development lies with the neighbouring Aeroplane and Armament Experimental Establishment at Boscombe Down. It began life as part of the Red House Farm, situated on Boscombe Down West, agricultural land used primarily for sheep. The area was requisitioned as an aerodrome in October 1917 and was initially known as Red House Farm Aerodrome, Royal Flying Corps. The name soon changed to the now familiar and more appropriate Boscombe Down.

The need for pilots and observers during the 1914-18 war produced a dramatic increase in training aerodromes, many of which were built on Salisbury Plain, joining the Upavon and Netheravon airfields and being served by the extensive military railway system extending out from Amesbury station.

Boscombe became the No 6 Training Depot Station, initially with tented accommodation for personnel and aeroplanes, the George Inn at Amesbury serving as the officers mess until suitable buildings were erected on the aerodrome. Completed in August 1918, Boscombe Down played a brief but important part in training airmen from the British, Colonial and American services, becoming redundant following the Armistice in November 1918. It spent the following two years as a storage unit and then, in May 1920 it was closed, reverting to farmland once more.

In 1926 the site was purchased by the Air Ministry and rebuilt as a bomber station, remaining principally with the newly formed Bomber Command until the outbreak of the 1939-45 war. The Aeroplane and Armament Experimental Establishment then arrived, hurriedly evacuated from its airfield on Martlesham Heath, and bringing sixty assorted aircraft to an aerodrome not initially having any of the required test facilities.

Boscombe Down became a very busy aerodrome during the war, with a staff of over 2000 servicemen which eventually resulted in additional accommodation being built between the airfield and Amesbury. Known as the Lower Camp Site, it subsequently became a caravan park and a MOD housing estate.

Post-war activities, particularly in the 1950's, largely followed the war-time pattern and intensity, the growing number of civilian employees having to be housed in Salisbury, Harnham and Amesbury - the latter on the newly-formed Solstice Farm council estate. Major civilianisation of the establishment occurred during the latter half of the 1950's resulting in an increasing requirement for more permanent accommodation with the gradual integration of more civilian personnel into the local community.

Boscombe Down, whilst sited largely within the parish of Amesbury but outside the curtilage of the town itself, has exercised a significant influence on Amesbury and the surrounding area. Although the sophistication and complexity of modern aircraft and technology inevitably produce changing work patterns and staffing levels, it will no doubt continue to maintain its presence and act as a major influence in the future.

The earlier character of the road between Amesbury and Boscombe can be seen in this illustration of 1915.

Holders Road Although it does not give access to the town, this is probably a convenient moment to consider Holders Road. It originally linked the east end of London Road with the road leading up from Amesbury to Boscombe Down. Now it gives access also to the various local authority estates along its route. Holders Road contains houses that are probably unique to Amesbury. Erected just after the 1914-18 war by the Ministry of Agriculture and Fisheries in conjunction with the Department of Scientific and Industrial Research the houses were intended as an experimental examination of various almost forgotten rural building methods and tests of new materials, techniques and apparatus.

The project resulted from the requirements of the Land Settlement Act and included with each house sufficient land for a small-holding, from which the road-name is derived. The holdings and dwellings were made available at a low annual rental for those returning from the war to train as farmers or smallholders. There were approximately 14 single houses and 18 pairs of cottages, utilising revived old methods, new methods and normal methods of the time. These included pisé de terre, chalk cob, weatherboard with timber frame, brick and concrete. Converted army sectional huts were also included in the scheme, to ensure that every avenue was explored.

Then and now - how the experimental houses and their environment in Holders Road have matured since 1920.

Sixty-nine years later the holdings have all but disappeared, lost under a sea of houses and amenity development; the last of the land still under cultivation is about to be overtaken by a similar fate. The houses, however, are all, apart from one, standing as firm as ever. That which is lost was vandalised after being left vacant. There is no building method yet devised that is immune to that particular process! It is rewarding to see that twelve of these dwellings, plus one in Ratfyn Road, have been included in the latest list of buildings of special architectural or historic interest.

Coldharbour in 1934. The cob-walled cottages are built along the centre of the old drove-way.

Coldharbour today - all the cottages are gone, only the bungalow at the right and the distant house at centre-right remaining from the previous photograph.

The Drove and Coldharbour   Of the two, the Drove appears to have appreciably earlier origins. Although now associated with just another building estate and with the right of common way reduced to a footpath's width, it was originally at least 150ft wide in places, enough for the vast flocks of sheep and cattle to be brought from the downs into the town market and beyond onto new pastures. The Drove is now identifiable from the point where it leaves Holders Road, just off the London Road. Its original width can be seen in the depth of the gardens plus the footpath and road of the same name. Entering Coldharbour from the east, the wide road was gradually encroached upon by the mud-walled cottages of vergeside squattings, later used by estate workers and tenants, erected on waste ground in the roadway during the 18th and 19th centuries and followed, early this century, by the infant school premises, bungalows and local authority dwellings, to become the metalled Coldharbour road of today. Both the Drove and adjacent Kitchener Road contained extensive allotment areas, evident here since the 19th century and only relatively recently declining in popularity, eventually becoming a housing development.

The London Road   The London Road, in common with Countess and Salisbury Roads, exhibits the "ribbon" development characteristics by which, during the early 20th century, a growing community was able to house its increasing populace, bringing with it the diversity of architectural styles established before the more formalised planning regulations evolved.

The earlier lack of planning control left the east end of London Road something of a disaster area with, up to ten years ago, decaying tin huts, a redundant petrol filling station and other utilitarian commercial establishments that blended to give the area a distinct second-rate impression. The large NAAFI complex overshadows the Folly Bottom approach, an unfortunate example of planning with complete disregard to the surrounding environment. Since that time the Amesbury Transport Company has also placed its stamp upon the scene, building massive warehouse premises which, when combined with its existing adjacent properties, places an additional and unmistakeable emphasis on the character of the area. In spite of this and other recent development plus the other commercial enterprises and the stated aims to make this an industrial area, no direct access to the west-bound A303 has yet been provided. Heavy goods vehicles still rumble down London Road and precariously negotiate the difficult crossroads in the town on to the A345 before eventually reaching the trunk road. An amazing omission! Consideration is being given at the moment to provide a link road from Folly Bottom around to the south of the town, a partial and very controversial solution. Thankfully the character of London Road does recover itself somewhat as one nears the town. The first notable inclusion on the scene is a series of now much modified single-storeyed flat-roofed bungalows. Built in eastern style during the 1920's by the local entrepreneur "Bungy" Woods of whom we have written earlier, they remain interesting examples of an early rural application of "reinforced" concrete. Mr Woods, always a resourceful man, collected together whatever metalwork he thought would be useful as a reinforcing agent, and it has

Bungy Wood's concrete bungalows, more officially described as "interesting Neo-Renaissance one-storey residences".

Two of the bungalows today; of the original number, some have been demolished, all now have pitched roofs, and one has had a second storey added.

been observed that this included various parts of early aircraft which in those days were readily available. The bungalows were originally built for a client who became bankrupt and Bungy, being the principal creditor, took them in part payment for what he was owed. Some of them have since been demolished, all now have pitched roofs and one has had a second storey added.

About half-way along the road one meets the easterly entrance to Lord's Walk, marked by a large tumulus now enclosed in an adjacent garden. Here also is the entrance to Ratfyn Road, an earlier main entrance to the town from the north; now a private road but with a public right of way that still permits access to the neighbouring village of Bulford along much the same route as before. Further along towards the town the site of Amesbury's Roman Catholic Church, founded in 1934, has recently undergone a transformation. Large-scale redevelopment has moved the church back from the road, with the "Cloisters" retirement apartments taking its place. The neighbouring YMCA establishment and associated garages, which replaced earlier cottages and other dwellings, have also gone, replaced in turn by yet another development of retirement apartments and bungalows which take up the whole of the corner site, spreading into Countess Road as far as the Druids Restaurant.

West

Access to Amesbury from the west has seen much modification over the years. Today one approaches on the A303 by-pass, passing, on the north side, the now rapidly decaying beech clumps once attractively positioned to represent the British and French ships at the Battle of the Nile in 1798. On the southern side is the Iron Age hillfort known erroneously as Vespasian's Camp.

Stonehenge Road   Prior to the construction of the by-pass in 1970, to enter the town from the west one would leave the present route of the A303 close to the first of the beech clumps and bear right, down the hill into the town, past the rather fine milestone which, bearing the date 1764 reminds one of the turnpike era. This portion of road now allows only one-way through traffic, permitting one to leave the town and to join the westbound A303; two-way traffic is resumed from the junction with the West Amesbury road. This area has gained the name of Gallows Hill, the exact reason in this particular case not being clear as no references have been found to substantiate the execution of local justice here. It has been speculated that the naming is derived from the memory of some local tragedy. The line taken by Stonehenge Road into Amesbury cuts through the west portion of Vespasian's Camp, with dwellings of diverse size and character set back from the road along its west bank.

Another, more localised, approach to Amesbury from the westerly direction is represented by the various rights of way from West Amesbury, Normanton and Durnford all of which cross the Avon at Ham Hatches, skirting the recreation

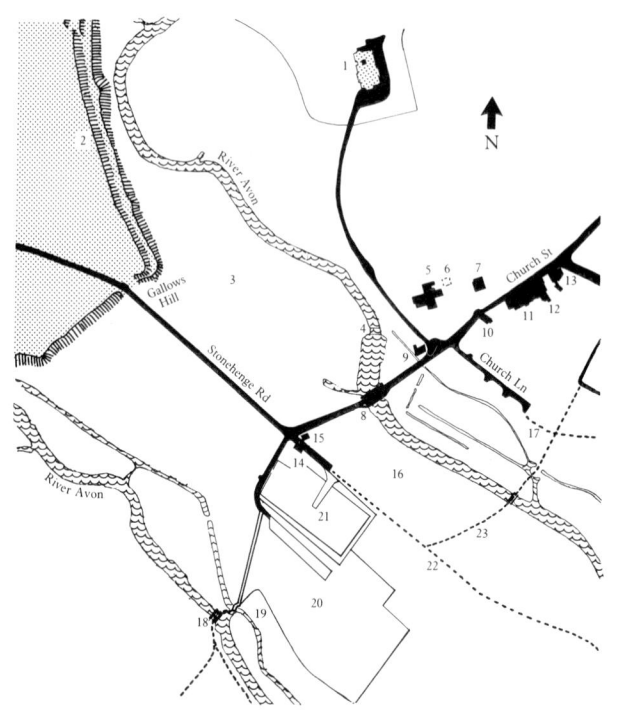

1 The Abbey Mansion and Park
2 Vespasian's Camp boundary
3 Water meadows
4 Queens Falls weir
5 Parish Church of St Mary and St Melor
6 Site of former vicarage
7 Present vicarage
8 Queensberry Bridge, or Great Bridge
9 Tumbling Bay
10 The Phoenix
11 Antrobus Arms Hotel (also former vicarage and school)
12 King's Arms Hotel
13 Lloyds Bank and site of former Market House
14 Little Thatch cottage
15 Site of toll-house
16 Water Meadows
17 Almanaze path
18 Ham hatches
19 Bonney Mead
20 Recreation Ground
21 Cemetery
22 Wittenham path
23 Approximate route of Broad Bridge road

ground along its northern edge and meeting the former turnpike road at Cemetery Corner. The importance of these paths has long since declined, belying their earlier busy nature. Once they would have permitted the labourers access to their strips of land, allowed the shepherd to drive sheep to the downs and seen much traffic to Dawbony's Mill which appears to have stood in the vicinity of Ham Hatches.

Up to the early part of the 17th century this entrance to the town appears to have continued in a southerly direction from Cemetery Corner. By 1675 a wooden bridge was constructed approximately on the site of the present stone bridge which superseded it in 1775, allowing the road to take its present line. The route of the earlier road can be seen in the line of the present Wittenham footpath, which has evolved from an 18th century access road. Following the footpath south for approximately 150 yards one would then turn eastwards, crossing the river at Broad Bridge, entering the town via Frog Lane. By the early 18th century the bridge was gone, remembered only by the field name which led to the river. While Broad Bridge existed it must have provided a principal westerly access to the town, possibly for cattle and sheep, its continuation to Frog Lane giving direct access to the market. This busy area could be avoided by through traffic, by branching right into the later Tanners Lane, the present southerly half of Flower Lane. The approach road to Broad Bridge became a cul-de-sac, giving access only to the fields and watermeadows. The shallowness of the river at that point permitted it to be forded, allowing continued use, with a more circuitous alternative using the Wood-Way from Durnford, to approach Amesbury along the west bank of the river from Ham Hatches around to South Mill. Additionally, a route may have existed to the north of Vespasian's Camp, joining Countess Road at some point as indicated by paths prior to the by-pass, but this is somewhat speculative. Many such lesser paths and spurs were yielded up by the Parish Council when the definitive map of rights of way was drawn up in 1948/50 and these were confirmed as no longer in use at the first review of the map in the 1950's.

West Amesbury Although situated to the west of the main town it actually lies on an earlier principal north-south route which follows the Avon, joining Stonehenge Road for its access to Amesbury. Its origin is obscure but appears to be centred around the Priory, with lands here being held by the Prioress of Amesbury in 1261 and by which it appears to have evolved as part of the Priory Manor. What one sees today is a picturesque hamlet separated from the town by the river and intervening high ground on which has been constructed the iron age fort. It contains mainly cottages, formerly dwellings of farm tenants, which have mostly made the costly transition into private ownership. Together with agricultural buildings they cluster around the principal building, West Amesbury House.

West Amesbury House: principally 16th to 17th century construction in chequer stone and flint; contains traces of an older building thought to have been associated with Amesbury's religious house.

Little is known about the earlier history of West Amesbury House. It has been much altered over the years, with evidence of 15th century origins and later work in the 17th, 18th and 20th centuries. It may have been associated with Amesbury's religious house and has been considered to be either a grange or infirmary.

The peaceful hamlet of West Amesbury has not changed in appearance much since the turn of the century, as these two illustrations show.

88

The western toll-house and adjacent cottage, formerly Pink House school, at the south end of Stonehenge Road. The principal route turns left, passing the front of the toll-house at the left of the picture. The former road continued between the two buildings and is now known as the Wittenham path.

Chapter 9

Amesbury Parish Church

Introduction

The church that we see today is a large building for a community of such relatively modest size. It is a building that has slowly evolved over the years into its present form and to do some sort of justice to its antiquity and character a detailed description has been attempted. A close inspection of the building will reveal the many alterations that have taken place and which reflect the changing demands made upon it over the centuries.

The church consists principally of a 12th century nave, with transepts, chapel, tower and chancel of mid 13th century date. Later work by the eminent Victorian architect William Butterfield resulting from his extensive restoration of the church in 1853, can also be seen. Further extensive restoration occurred early in this century, with repairs to roofs and floors, the crossing piers and the south aisle, plus underpinning and ventilation of the foundations. In addition to its role as a place of Christian worship it has been meeting place, school, refuge and store and still stands today as an example of the highest aspirations of this little community. Its precise link with the monastic house, remains of which were found at the west end of the nave and several hundred yards to the north, is still an unanswered question but the proximity in the 18th century of a water mill and several other large buildings of agricultural nature lends substance to the theory that it may have evolved from some connection with the monastic church, later becoming that of the parish as well. This uncertainty has communicated itself at times to the title, it being for a period altered to Amesbury Abbey Church. However, with no new evidence of a definitive link with the abbey brought forward, the title has once again reverted to the dedication to St Mary and St Melor.

One's first impression is of a church built principally from stone and flint on the Latin cross plan with a central crossing tower which dominates not so much by its height but by its massive proportions. Add to it the octagonal spire which may have adorned the tower until the dissolution, and add the other missing portions to the church and one has a building not unimpressive in size and complexity. The traditional steep pitch of the original roof, so well designed for the prevailing weather conditions, can be seen by the slope of the roof line mouldings above the present tiles. As lead came more into use from the 13th century onwards, the steep pitch was reduced to that seen in the nave roof to avoid the tendency of the sheet metal to 'creep'; although the former eaves have been retained, the more normal parapet which one might have expected was not incorporated for some reason. Later work restored the pitch of the transept and chancel roofs. At the south-west side of the church, let into the boundary wall, one can see the shed or outhouse, constructed from many of the parts that Butterfield found surplus or which did not fit his scheme. Left with just a pile of stones he chose a hopefully redeeming action! The wall itself is worth just a mention. Half way along, near the war memorial, a discontinuity formed by stone blocks and resembling quoins can be seen. This feature relates quite accurately in position to the corner of one of the large buildings shown on the 1726 map of the town. Hence it is possible that the portion of this wall towards the church formed the lower part of an earlier east wall of quite a sizeable building - possibly a tithe barn.

The Exterior

To look at the church more closely, walk around the outside, starting at the present main entrance, the south transept door.

The South Transept The present south face of this transept was designed by Butterfield who did so much either to enhance the building, or to degrade it if the Victorian Gothic style does not appeal.

Up to 1853, when the alterations were made, this south face was constructed in the Renaissance style and contained a door positioned much as the present one, a single lancet window centrally above, with a circular opening over that, the whole being surmounted by the sundial that is retained. This former facade originated in 1721.

The church prior to its restoration by Butterfield. This 18th century view also shows the former vicarage, now demolished, which was thought to be part of the monastic buildings. The fence was removed by the Turnpike Trust in 1826 when the road was widened.

The east wall of the south transept shows the former existence of another chapel, illustrated by the roof line and the blocked arch now pierced by a 15th century three-light cusped window. The misalignment between the roof moulding and the arch is curious, suggesting two different periods of use, the arch tending to align with the grooving in the angle buttress of the tower and hence perhaps being the later of the two features, neither of which have ever received an adequate explanation. The alignment of the 15th century window inserted in the blocked arch suggests it was either the product of hasty workmanship or outward pressure from the weight of the tower, the jamb and mullions having strayed noticeably from the vertical. A lancet window serves to break the monotony of the remainder of this wall and is the survivor of two, the other being blocked in the opposite wall.

Continuing around the church in a westerly direction, one can see on the west wall of the south transept much evidence of the periodic repair and patching that has taken place over the years. The blocked 13th century lancet window has given way to an 18th century "Classical" version, which has itself been blocked with flint. The possibility that the Romanesque building incorporated transepts that were reworked into the later 13th century structure may be suggested by the 12th century flat buttress now partially concealed at the corner made by the transept and south aisle.

The south-east aspect of the church as it appears today. Some of the 19th century alterations made to the chancel and south transept can be seen, by comparison with the previous illustration.

In this view from the north-west the former roof-lines are clearly visible on the tower walls, as is the string-course in the nave north wall.

The South Aisle The south side along the length of the nave is in the late 15th century Perpendicular style, the irregularities in the window masonry again exhibiting signs of inexperience or hasty execution in the task of insertion. The large Tudor style door at the west end was, until the 19th century, under the cover of a large stone porch of late medieval period, or later.

The west end of the church is reached through the gate in the wall.

The Nave At the west end of the church one can see again the evidence of much change. The west wall of the nave is by Butterfield, his windows replacing an earlier three-light Perpendicular window. On the upper portion of the nave west wall, before it joins the south aisle, one can see the several dripstone lines left without a function as a result of progressive alteration. The position of the portion of richly shafted 12th or early 13th century doorway protruding from the west end of the nave may be misleading as it is possibly reset. As presently orientated its use as an entrance would take one away from the nave. Excavations in 1920 established what were thought to be Saxon door footings aligned with, but about a foot away from, the nave north wall. Recent work, in 1978, has shown them to be of a later period, and positioned at an angle of about 5° to the nave, suggesting a separate building to the present structure.

Continuing round the end of the nave to its north wall, further evidence of the Norman period can be seen in the weather-worn corbel table under the eaves and also in the blocked window arches. The two existing windows are in the later

Perpendicular style. The unfortunate but main feature of this wall is the Victorian "crazy-paving" effect which, as elsewhere on the building, Butterfield seems to have achieved with lasting brilliance.

The horizontal moulded course running along the wall at mid-height has been thought to provide evidence of former cloisters. If the slope of the string course on the north transept wall is considered it seems more probable that a 12th century passage of the "lean-to" style is suggested, or possibly but more unlikely a north aisle. Cloisters, if any, might have led off from such an aisle if positioned in the usual monastic configuration. The positioning of the later windows high in the wall would suggest the continuing presence of a structure along the north side until the 15th or even 16th century when it might have been demolished at the dissolution.

The North Transept   The north and west walls of the north transept are mid 13th century in general character and again possess the typically graceful lancet windows of that period. The blocked door in the west wall gives an indication of former passage between the supposed north structure and the interior. Evidence of other former structures, long since disappeared and of unknown purpose, is given by the still visible quoin stones set into the west wall at the transept north-west corner, and by the roll-moulding along the north end, running through the window bases. The east wall of the transept provides a slightly more exciting prospect, apart from the classical lines of the lean-to tool shed. The predominant feature in this wall is the Jesus Chapel, of slightly later date than the main structure as suggested by the partially concealed roll-moulding that runs around the north end of the transept. The lower windows of the chapel are Early English lancets but the upper window in the gable is a more ornate affair of plate tracery, with two trefoil-headed lights divided by a small pillar with foliated capital and with a quatrefoil opening in its head. It has been dated as 14th century and is thought to be reset.

Close to the chancel wall is Butterfield's brick and sandstone gothic style turret staircase, surmounted by its fine wrought-iron cross enriched with blacksmith's scrollwork. The turret replaces the earlier interior staircase and leads to the ringing floor of the bell-tower. An external access has apparently been bricked up. Partially obscured by the turret is the blocked archway with roof moulding that would have led from the north transept to a side chapel or vestry for the chancel. This vestry has, of course, long since disappeared but ample evidence remains; for instance, the blocked lower portions of the 13th century lancet windows and the blocked 13th century door with its nearby aumbry or cupboard, now just a niche in the wall.

The Chancel   The presence of the Decorated window in the north wall, inserted during the first quarter of the 14th century, suggests that the chancel side chapel, or vestry, had possibly gone by that time. The fact that this window is not aligned with the one of similar period in the south wall may also suggest that the easterly part of the vestry remained at that time. The window is of interesting style, being a fine example of reticulated tracery. It is possible that it was executed by a west country mason, as he introduced into the corbels at the foot of the interior arch the ball-flower ornament so popular in Gloucestershire and Somerset during this period. Little other work of the 14th century remains in the church, having been mostly discarded by Butterfield. An angle or 'French' buttress exists at the north-east corner of the chancel, a variation not introduced to England until the 14th century. It was built probably at the time that the aisle was removed. The remaining buttresses on this side date from the Victorian period and became necessary only then to lend support to the bulging chancel walls. The east end of the chancel received attention from Butterfield during his restoration work of 1853. Prior to this time the east wall contained a large five-light Perpendicular window attributed to the 15th century period. For reasons unknown but presumably its poor condition, it was replaced by the window present today. It must be said in Butterfield's favour that he appears to have retained the ashlar face and to have effected this part of his work without scarring the overall character too deeply.

Continuing on round the building, the same architectural theme is present in the south face of the chancel, the ashlar work in the upper part this time contrasting with the lower rubble walling that would have originally been plastered over, not coming into favour in its own right until the 19th century.

The line of the graceful 13th century lancet windows in the south wall is broken by the later insertion of the Decorated window, of slightly earlier style than that in the north wall. This one is a rather nice example of cusped intersected tracery, with a large pointed quatrefoil spreading out at the top. A priests' door was removed from the centre of this wall in the 19th century and the jamb incorporated either in the verger's shed or in the wall around the present vicarage, the doors in these two structures being sufficiently similar in general shape to make identification difficult from the rather vague drawings that exist.

The Interior

The South Transept Entering the church by the south transept door, now the principal entrance, there is, to one's left, the 15th century clock mechanism, in use until the early part of this century. A few years ago the chiming cylinder, or carillon, associated with the clock came to light in Oxford and was offered to Amesbury but without response. The barrel vault or wagon roof is of the Tudor period, as are those of the north transept and south aisle.

The South Aisle Passing along the transept and turning left into the south aisle, one can see the richly decorated roof, executed to great effect. Here also is the font, the upper portion of which is 12th or early 13th century Purbeck marble with the typical shallow blind arch decoration, reset on a 15th century arcaded limestone base. This font was broken up by Butterfield and used as rubble beneath the chancel floor, from whence it was recovered during later work at the beginning of this century and used to replace the Victorian version which is thought to have been acquired by one of the neighbouring village churches. In the south wall of the aisle, close to the font, is a small piscina with credence shelf, a relic from a former chapel or side altar. Close examination will reveal a particularly naïve interpretation in the heads forming the hoodmould stops, as if executed by an inexperienced mason. Another piscina, or stoup, now containing a medieval queen's head exists in the south wall close to the west door. Nearby is the only locally remaining medieval item retrieved from the excavations at the abbey in 1860, which brought to light the controversial remains of the monastic house. Described variously as font or lavatorium, with the former favoured, its date and precise purpose remain in doubt still.

The south aisle.

The Nave Standing at the west end of the nave gives one an idea of the spacious character of the building, particularly if the presence of a former north structure and a nave with its north and south walls pierced with archways is visualised. Further evidence of a north aisle of some sort is suggested by the 12th century pier with earlier base found deep in the north wall at the the east end of the nave during the 1920 repairs. The alignment of the pier is of interest as it does not conform to that of the present nave, but more with that of the chancel which can be seen to be well out of alignment with the nave when viewed from the west end.

The 12th century south wall is pierced by a 15th century two-bay arcade, leading to a south aisle of the same period. The recent arcade probably replaces an earlier version which formed part of the Norman nave, possibly balanced by a similar structure on the north side, the character being perhaps demonstrated by the base set into the north wall. In the upper part of the south wall can be seen the blocked Norman clerestory windows which once, before the present aisle was built, would have helped to illuminate an otherwise gloomy nave. Construction of the aisle, with the insertion of these two arches produced stress problems that had not been envisaged by the relatively rudimentary approach to the task. The south-west pier supporting the tower could no longer take the strain and showed its protest by leaning ominously. Support had to be provided rather hastily, which resulted in the rather ungainly rectangular addition to this pier. The departure of the tower pier from the vertical can best be seen by viewing it from the west end of the nave, looking towards the chancel and aligning it with the south-east pier, or other verticals. The supporting structure has been used to some alternative benefit, as can be seen from the remains of the late medieval wall-painting on the north face. Thought to represent Saint Melor, it has been reduced by the ravages of time and the application of much whitewash from a full-length figure, visible at the turn of the century, to the present barely discernible head and shoulders. Such little interest continues to be shown in its conservation or protection that before long it will probably disappear completely under a fresh coat of zealously applied paint! Other decorative points of interest in the nave are the photographs of the 'Amesbury Psalter' on the south wall and the hatchment depicting the coat of arms of the Antrobus family, for Sir Edmund Antrobus who died in 1870.

The late 15th-16th century timbers of the nave roof have moulded tie-beam trusses with open panelwork and carved wall brackets. Whilst elaborate, they do have a somewhat makeshift appearance suggesting that the roof was re-erected from various pieces, after the dissolution. This possibility is illustrated by the spacing of the wall corbels, which are positioned awkwardly in relation to the blocked windows on the north side. Additionally, poppy heads are broken from some of the cusps, poor carving is mixed with good and the filling of several of the spandrels is clumsy, differing from the original design.

Before the 19th century restoration the nave contained three galleries, the inferred dimensions of which must have appreciably restricted the space available to the devout community! The largest gallery was situated at the west end of the nave, more or less where the organ is currently positioned. It is recorded as projecting far into the church and having a front painted in black and white stripes. The space beneath was boarded up and used to hoard lumber and, in later years around the mid 19th century, used as a school. If normal convention was followed, this gallery was probably used by the local musicians, before the advent of the organ. Certainly if the lord of the manor and his guests were in the habit of attending the services a sizeable and relatively proficient orchestra would presumably be expected. Butterfield's restoration converted the area into a vestry.

Complementing, or competing with the band of musicians, would be the choir, which was housed in a sky-blue painted gallery of panelled deal, built in 1737 and situated in the easterly of the two archways between the nave and south aisle. It was considered by some to be a clumsy and disfiguring projection. Immediately to the west of this, presumably in the other archway, was an older, private gallery. This was apparently finished in a peach-blossom colour, lighted by white stripes.

At that time, the original pulpit, not the present 19th century one, stood complete with massive sounding board against the north-west pier of the tower arch. The pulpit was accompanied by the prayer desk and clerk's seat.

The interior of the church as intended by Butterfield. A spacious arch leading into the chancel with its typically Victorian tiles behind the altar.

A present-day view of the main body of the interior. The 15th century chancel screen, rescued from destruction, can be seen.

Butterfield's vestry at the west end of the nave has been dismantled to become the unfortunate site of the latest organ. The present organ was acquired from St Edmund's Church, Salisbury, in 1983 and replaced the two-manual electro-pneumatic organ built in 1888 by Alfred Monk of Camden Town for £280. The Monk organ was the latest technology of its time, the action being first used in England in 1868. Its principal advantage was that it permitted a new lightness of touch to the hitherto hard-pressed organist. It was carefully sited in the church, being placed unobtrusively and for the best acoustic effect. Unfortunately for Amesbury, the innovative technology was in some ways ahead of its time, as far as suitable long-lasting materials were concerned, and inevitably, over the years, the organ's condition was allowed to deteriorate to a point where major work was necessary, which could not be supported. It is, in a way, fortuitous that at that time the organ from the redundant church of St Edmund should become available. It is also sad that Amesbury's organ which had served so well for many years was only fit for scrap, disposed of with such undignified haste. A small portion apparently lives on in a Weymouth church. The new organ was built by one Charles Green, who had premises in Salisbury, and was first used in St Edmund's on Christmas Day 1777. In 1781 Henry Coster, a pupil of Charles Green, incorporated additional stops. In 1867 it was removed to the London firm of J Walker, where the manual compasses were extended, a swell box inserted, a choir incorporated and a pedal organ introduced. As seen today, the instrument is basically a three manual organ, with choir, swell and great, plus couplers and pedal. It is tracker action throughout, except for the pedals which are pneumatic.

The Jesus Chapel, the last remaining side chapel, is situated in the north transept.

The Norman font, reconstructed from fragments discovered under the chancel floor.

The North Transept The north transept is entered under the now defunct organ loft. Passing into the north transept one can see on the east wall, half hidden by the remaining screen, the blocked arch of the demolished chapel or vestry. The character of the arch is early 13th century, incorporating the typical moulded capitals on their stiff-leaf stops. Similar characteristics are to be seen at the entrance to the one chapel that still remains. The rib-vaulting rising from the slender shafts has foliated caps on the eastern side; there is also a double piscina, again with the stiff-leaf foliation at the hoodmould stops. Traces of red decorative line-work can still just be seen on the stonework in and around the piscina. The cross on the altar is made from oak beams recovered from the foundations during the 19th century work. Traces of a former entrance screen can be seen in the fixing points still visible in the pillars. The north transept was used in the 19th century for the storage of ladders and the fire appliance invented by the Reverend Thomas Holland, in addition to its more usual purpose. Emerging from the north transept, the wooden pulpit with stone base, to one's left, is of Butterfield's Victorian design.

The Chancel The chancel is entered through a 15th century five-light wooden screen. Much defaced and repaired, the screen has lost the rood-loft that it appears to have once supported. The screen was removed at the time of the 19th century restoration work, but rescued from the scrap-heap by Job Edwards, one of Amesbury's former historians, who kept it safe for many years until it could be replaced in 1907. To Butterfield, the chancel was the richest part and the focal point of a church. Screens were removed to make it visible; he made its roof the highest in the church and usually removed all side altars so that a chancel contained the only one. He appears to have relaxed this rule for Amesbury.

The fragments of coloured glass-work in the large windows of the north wall are mostly random pieces. The upper part of a fine 14th or 15th century Queen of Heaven has been preserved intact. An alternative theory suggests that it could depict Guinevere. The remaining fragments of stained glass are of various dates and include 13th or 14th century hatched grisaille pieces and Lombardic lettering, plus a small 16th century quarry below the top trefoil.

To the north of the altar is the interior portion of the blocked doorway, which is also visible from the outside, with its hoodmould and characteristic stiff-leaf stops. Here also is a small but unusually ornate recess, of the early to mid-14th century period. Canopied and crocketed, with openwork cusping and buttress shafts, it retains the Decorated feeling but exhibits inferior workmanship. It has been postulated that the clumsy design and poor carving resulted from the dearth of competent and progressive masons following the Black Death. If true, this might also account for the crude carving on the piscina near the font.

Behind the altar, Butterfield's tiling and marble panelling remain painted over and hidden from view by wall hangings. Perhaps one day, when the work of his period becomes more acceptable to Amesbury, it will again be exposed for all to see. To the south of the altar, the credence table is supported by the external hoodmould stops from the Perpendicular east window removed in the 19th century. The stops take the form of angels bearing carved escutcheons on which are worked in red and black clay the initials D K D interlaced with a cord. The principal initial K has been linked with the name Kent as there was, among the buildings of the monastery, an apartment known as Kent's chamber. According to the Reverend Ruddle, the canopied manor pew was situated at the south side of the chancel, just within the screen. The chancel walls at this point today bear the memorial tablets to members of the Antrobus family, the last and current manorial holders. A continuation of the now fading decorative red lining can be seen very faintly on the upper stonework surface of the south wall. The stained glass in the south-east lancet windows is of relatively recent date. The roof was restored by Butterfield to the original 13th century pitch.

The Tower The crossing tower is supported by four triple-chamfered arches. The south-west pier differs from the others, having a late medieval panel embellishment. A scratched symbol, suggesting a merchant's mark, is repeated on some of the stonework.

The Saxon Cross The cross was recovered from under the chancel floor during restoration work in 1907. Its site when found has been taken to suggest that it was one of the many items discarded by Butterfield during his restoration of the church, but there are at least two alternatives. It is possible from the siting that the cross was destroyed during work on the chancel in the 15th century, or, it could have been destroyed earlier if the present chancel is a rebuilding of a post-Saxon one contemporary with the remains of the 12th century nave. In

A most important body of men - the bell ringers.

The Saxon cross fragments.

102

considering its origin, it has been suggested that the cross could be from a 'minster' on the site of the present church, or that this could even be the site of the abbey founded in c.979. Its weathered condition suggests that it was an external feature, but it does not appear on any pre-restoration illustrations of the church, leading one still further to think that it may have been associated with an earlier structure. The fact that does remain is that the crosshead was associated with a Saxon church. It has been dated from the 9th to the 11th centuries but a more recent study of its characteristics suggests a date in the second half of the 10th century, a period contemporary with the first recorded founding of the abbey.

The wheelhead cross evolved in the Irish Sea cultural region and became the dominant form of cross there during the 10th and 11th centuries. In England its spread is initially associated with the Norse penetration of the north-west from Ireland and from there it spread across the Pennines into the Danish area. Its appearance in south and south-east England is rare. The wheelhead form of cross could have reached Amesbury overland from the north-west or, as is more likely, direct by sea via the Bristol Channel. There is, then, a suggestion at Amesbury of cultural links with Ireland during the mid or latter part of the 10th century.

The shape of the cross is a later form of the Anglian cross evolved in Northumbria at the turn of the 8th century. Elements of the design in the termination of the arms suggest an influence by a tradition exclusive to Ireland. The only two extant crosses with the identical pattern of linked triquetras are at Cardynham in Cornwall and Coychurch in Mid-Glamorgan. The interlace pattern around the edge of the head originated in northern Italy in the 9th century and is similar to that found on stones at nearby Ramsbury and at Wherwell. This fixes the earliest possible date for the Amesbury cross in the mid-9th century. The design and execution of the Amesbury cross are of a high quality, suggesting a competent sculptor, worthy to be employed by a rich patron with possible royal connections. An abbey was founded at Wherwell in 986 by Queen Aelfthryth, the foundress of Amesbury. It is interesting to note that all the sculptures in this group have been assigned dates prior to the known foundation of churches at each of the sites. Ties with the Celtic west could have survived here until the 10th century and perhaps this is reflected in the later dedication of Amesbury's church to Saint Melor. The cross may well represent Amesbury's earliest link with Christianity.

The cross is now rather poorly displayed in its glass case at the west end of the nave and has, in the last ten years, suffered some deterioration.

Bosses and Corbels Before leaving the church the corbels and ceiling bosses merit examination, if the neck and spine will permit! A mirror, plus a powerful torch and a pair of binoculars will also help.

The nave roof is supported at its corners by four corbels that take the shape of human figures who are obviously, from their facial expressions, aware of the serious nature of their task in keeping the woodwork in its rightful place. Here also is Abraham, releasing the ram from the bush; a cardinal and a bishop thought to represent Cardinal Carpaccio and Bishop Beauchamp, 14th century figures.

Grotesquely carved roof bosses, such as those shown here, served to remind wayward members of the congregation of the perils that awaited if their attentions should wander. Other carvings depicted local worthies, legendary figures and biblical scenes.

Nearby a regal figure, possibly either King Arthur or Ambrosius Aurelianus appears close to the west end. Of the bosses in the woodwork, there is some floral decoration and a horned devil emitting tongues of flame. The corbels and bosses in the south aisle can be more plainly seen; humorously grotesque heads, human figures and flowers. In the south transept are knights - possibly one-time benefactors or local persons; a monster head devouring a man grimly represents Judas Iscariot in the jaws of Satan; another, equally menacing head, grips a large bone between its prominent teeth. The faithful few were left in no doubt of the fate that would befall them if they transgressed! In the north transept religious practices have been conducted on a much more formal basis, under the watchful and uniform gaze of six disapproving angels clutching escutcheons.

Conclusions

As we have seen, the building has been subjected to much modification over the years, some of which, as dictated by the architectural styles imposed, tend to coincide with the known periods of rebuilding or alteration in the monastic house. Apart from the nave, the dimensions given for the roofs that were stripped of lead at the time of the dissolution agree fairly well with the relevant dimensions in the present church. One hypothesis is that the nave belonged to the parish but that the crossing and chancel were rebuilt in the 13th century to accommodate the male canons introduced by the Order of Fontevrault to form a joint community. The reason for the removal of the structures on the north side of the church is not known but it appears to have occurred prior to the 15th century, in which period a change of use, or emphasis, seems to have taken place, with the main access to the church being transferred to the south side. This is perhaps connected with the removal of the brethren and the severing of links with France. A move is possibly reflected by the absence of any graves 'behind' the present church and the earliest graves around the present front appearing, as far as can be ascertained, not to pre-date this period.

So, until further evidence comes to light, the precise relationship of the present church to the abbey must remain unresolved. The questions prompted by the discovery of the remains 300 yards to the north, that have troubled scholars over the last hundred years must still remain unanswered. One can only say that the size and characteristics of the building, including the now missing portions, seem to suggest some sort of monastic connection, it appearing too large for just a simple town church.

Chapter 10

The Central Area

When we examined the approaches to Amesbury, we ended up at the west side of the town. We can start our look at the central area from that point, and begin at the bottom, or west end, of Church Street. Before launching into that account, however, we can use the location with the river, recreation ground and nearby downland, to consider briefly the sporting and leisure activities of the townspeople.

Recreation

As we have seen earlier, up to the 19th century the ordinary man led a very hard life. Such social events that occurred during the year must have been very welcome and anticipated with a degree of excitement that is largely lost today. The most important event of the year was the annual fair, held around Michaelmas, at which labourers were engaged or discharged from their employment, and livestock was bought and sold. Farmers, labourers, tenants and all would have come to these events from all the surrounding villages to buy, sell or just to gossip and meet friends. No doubt Amesbury would have been packed on such occasions. Earlier, in the medieval period, these events would have included activities of a different nature, with archery practice and other militaristic pastimes. This is reflected in the field named "les Butts". Its precise location is not known but appears to have been around the north side of the manor park where, since the 17th century, the annual fair on Countess Court Fields was held. The site of this event spread to Stonehenge, and the Cursus to its north, it being one of four similar events held through the year. In addition there were weekly markets held in or adjacent to the town.

By the beginning of the 20th century the fairs and markets had diminished both in number and importance. As social events they had to some extent been replaced by the various sporting pastimes practised. Sporting and leisure activities pursued locally are not really recorded until the 18th century but there is little doubt that what amused the inhabitants here was no different from the general scene elsewhere.

Prior to the Victorian period, available leisure time would have been mostly confined to a Sunday and, from the late 18th century onwards, could well have been spent near Stonehenge watching or playing in the cricket, football and golf matches that were held there until the early part of the 20th century. The downs from Stonehenge to Beacon Hill were also the scene of coursing meetings, the nationally popular sport prior to fox-hunting. Amesbury boasted the second club to be founded in Wiltshire and such was its fame that the meetings attracted participants from as far afield as Altcar in Lancashire. So highly prized were the dogs that those superior in the chase were even immortalised in verse. Fishing has also been long established but the present sport stops short of the 18th century fashion for young loach to be swallowed live with a glass of sack! The river was regarded as a useful source of food until well into the 20th century when it was even then periodically dragged with nets to catch the fish and eels.

Recreational activities were often spontaneous affairs dictated by circumstances, as seen here in 1909 on the frozen river at Lords Walk.

Not quite sport, but the 1910 elections allowed a certain freedom of expression! An interesting point here is the continuation from medieval times of the hobby-horse theme, now largely lost.

National matters could also produce a joyous response as seen in this procession celebrating the 1911 coronation.

By the mid 20th century fox-hunting had waned, coursing was extinct and recreational pursuits had evolved conforming more to the requirements of the working person. A recreation ground was provided for the public by the Parish Council in the 1920's and now more use was being made of it for the more organised games of football, cricket and tennis. It was also the home of the annual carnival, except when this was held in the abbey grounds, and the annual flower and produce show, these occasions acting to some extent as replacements for the centuries-old fairs.

The carnival took place on the Saturday nearest to mid-summer day, the 24th of June. Attempts to revive this event in the 1950's faltered and the Amesbury Parish (now Town) Council agreed to underwrite it, but fortunately this help was only needed for a short period. The carnival committee rallied and now raises substantial sums each year which are returned to community causes.

The annual flower show gave the local gardeners the chance of competing with one another to produce the best fruit, vegetables and flowers from their own gardens. A show was held each August Bank Holiday Monday. The first remembered was in 1923 and, in 1939, the last one before the 1939-45 war was held. The show was revived in 1955 and kept going until 1959. The change in the use of leisure time, the influence of television, the more readily available produce from newly emerging stores and supermarkets and the demise of the garden allotments caused interest in gardening to decline and it became impossible to provide the necessary committee. Exhibitors declined in numbers and shows became a repetition of the same names each year and now even this outlet of self-expression is gone.

The recreation ground still lives on and, although some of its usefulness has been replaced by the provision of newer facilities at the Holders Road sports centre, it still remains the only location that can cater for the public cricket and football matches played regularly and is still a venue for families with young children. It is a great pity that some of its former scenic qualities are lacking, through the ravages of Dutch Elm disease and the demands of modern usage.

Stonehenge was a natural venue for many social gatherings, although it is believed that on this occasion the purpose was to protest about its impending sale.

Amesbury Town Band The town band also holds a significant place in Amesbury's recreational activities. Its early history is a little uncertain as more than one appear to have existed from time to time and no definitive record exists.

The present band appears to have its origins in the Amesbury Temperance Brass Band thought to have been formed in 1905. Prior to that an Amesbury Fife and Drum Band existed, which was formed about 1868 and which around ten years later became the Amesbury Town Brass Band. In 1889 a second fife and drum band was formed but this one appears to have been disbanded about four years later, with members joining the Amesbury Town Brass Band. These bands were important features at fêtes, flower shows and garden parties. A particular event recorded is a parade through the streets, marking the relief of Kimberley and Ladysmith during the Boer War.

The brass band continued until about 1903, when interest began to wane, but it managed to keep going until at least 1912. The Temperance Brass Band was still in existence and apparently making modest progress, eventually amalgamating with the Town Brass Band, the two continuing together until the first world war.

Following the war, attempts were made to reform a band; it was found that many former members had been killed in the war or did not wish to take up playing again. However, a band was formed which managed to continue under various leaders until 1930 when new silver-plated instruments were purchased at a cost of £300, to replace the ageing brass ones. This period seems to have produced a regeneration of interest, the band travelling and performing at events all over the Wessex area, including concerts, parades and contests, a particular local event being the midsummer Druidical ceremonies at Stonehenge. The band also hosted a midsummer contest for a number of years until the second world war, attracting contestants from all over the Wessex Association area. The war interrupted activities; instruments were called in and stored until hostilities ceased. After the war, the band started up again, its activities continuing through the 1950's with many contest successes. In the mid-1960's interest again began to diminish, to a point where the band more or less ceased to exist.

It was reformed as the Amesbury Town Silver Band in 1969, from which date it has continued successfully, playing at local and more distant venues. A particular occasion remembered is that of playing before Prince Charles during Amesbury's millennium celebrations.

The earliest photograph of Amesbury's band that has been found - so far. Thought to have been taken around 1900, it appears to show links with the Ancient Order of Foresters.

The band in 1937, with its new instruments.

Church Street

Starting at the westerly end, we have today the thatched cottage originally built on Boney Mead and known in the 19th century as "Pink House". The former preparatory school for Rose's Grammar School, it was run by a Miss Mary Sandell in 1821 and by her successors. Until about 1920 it was accompanied by the westerly of Amesbury's tollhouses, which was situated on the east side of the Wittenham path. Near here also were the wooden hutted offices of Bungy Woods' gravel pits, with the narrow gauge railway leading away to the south alongside the path to the gravel pits next to the present effluent disposal plant.

The western end of Church Street, leading to Stonehenge Road, the cemetery and the recreation ground. The toll-house, the nearer of the two buildings, was demolished by a runaway vehicle in the late 1920's or early 1930's. The other building, Pink House cottage - or Little Thatch as it is currently named - still stands. It is interesting to note the line of the fencing which, until well into this century, ran at an angle to the road as it approached the river, a reminder of the way to the earlier ford and animal crossing. The boundary line has been moved in more recent years to run parallel with the edge of the road.

Proceeding towards the town centre the stone bridge, known as the Queensberry bridge, is crossed. As we saw earlier, when it was built by John Smeaton in 1775, following the institution of the turnpikes, access to Amesbury from the west was greatly facilitated. A little further along the street, by the small stone bridge carrying a former mill leet, later to be used to control the water meadows as well, is the most recent of the abbey park gatehouses. Used as such until relatively recently, its introduction followed construction of the southern entrance to the park in the mid 18th century. The gate piers with their Tuscan half columns forming the entrance to the park, are thought to be 17th century and were moved to the present site from nearer the former abbey mansion during the mid-18th century. The red-brick lodge occupies a site close to where a mill and

111

tanyards existed during the 18th century. Until the mid-1960's hatches and eel-traps existed where now can be seen the Queen's Falls weir. In addition to the mill several buildings of quite large dimension existed here during the 18th century, adjacent to the river and the church, possibly part of the earlier monastic buildings complex.

The Great Bridge, otherwise Queensberry Bridge, from a 19th century engraving.

The title of Abbey is possessed today by the 19th century mansion and its surrounding parkland which is much reduced from the acreage of former years. Following the dissolution, Amesbury estates were granted to Edward Seymour, who was created Earl of Hertford. During the period 1541 to 1543 the earlier monastic buildings were partially demolished. Edward was eventually accused of treason, and beheaded, his estates having been confiscated. His son, Edward, was restored to favour by Queen Elizabeth I and later regained the property at Amesbury by which time it was, apparently, in a poor condition. He leased it out, with promises to repair it. Edward was in turn succeeded by his son William who, after difficult times himself, was created Marquess of Hertford in 1640. The Seymour property was seized by the State during the Interregnum, the abbey and grounds again being let to a tenant. After distinguished service on the Royalist side in the civil war, William was restored to the Dukedom in September 1660 and died in October of that year. Before his death he employed the architect John Webb, nephew and pupil of Inigo Jones, to build a new house. Webb's house was built on the site of the priory and lasted for 173 years, having wings added during the mid 18th century and other more minor alterations undertaken at various other times. It gained both praise and criticism for its style.

The Amesbury estate eventually came into the ownership of Henry Boyle, Lord Carleton, Chancellor of the Exchequer, in 1720. On his death the house and estate were bequeathed to Charles Douglas 3rd Duke of Queensberry. The Duke and Duchess took up residence in 1729 following their patronage of the poet John Gay. Enlargements to the house were carried out by Henry Flitcroft, the adjacent iron age hill-fort known as "Vespasian's Camp" was purchased and Charles Bridgeman employed to landscape the gardens and provide a deer park.

The Abbey Mansion in the early 19th century.

The Abbey mansion today.

The 3rd Duke died in 1778 and was succeeded by the 4th Duke of Queensberry. He was only an occasional user of the house, taking away some of the furnishings and allowing the grounds to become overgrown. Various items of work on the house were carried out during his time by a George Parsons of Amesbury. Following the death of the 4th Duke in 1810, the abbey passed to Archibald, Lord Douglas of Douglas. It was eventually purchased in 1824, apparently in a poor state, by Sir Edmund Antrobus. A grandiose rebuilding of the Webb house by the fashionable and self-taught architect Thomas Hopper began in 1834. Hopper did not produce an entirely new building, his work being to some extent an enlargement and renovation of Webb's house, incorporating some of the original walls and 18th century fittings. The Palladian style he adopted was intended to reflect the earlier Webb design. The house one sees today is Hopper's and consists of three storeys and attic executed in Chilmark stone, built around a central space with arcaded galleries on the first and second floors. As originally conceived this present house had a sizeable ballroom along the south front and an imposing dining room in the 17th century style on the east side. Hopper was also able to take advantage of the modern technology of his time and incorporate steel beams and large plate-glass windows into the design. The mansion remained the property of the Antrobus family until 1979, its interior in recent years being divided into flats. It has since undergone conversion into a private nursing home. Existence of earlier monastic buildings on the same site was proven when, in 1860, excavations were made to the rear of the house for the purpose of adding servants' quarters. Wall and pillar footings, tiled flooring and other items of carved stonework were brought to light. Crop markings, noticed during the very dry summer of 1870 suggested the existence of further foundations to the east of the mansion, along the riverside towards Kent House. This tradition has never been substantiated and may only be evidence of the former 18th century formal gardens which are thought to have existed to the east of the house.

Opposite the abbey entrance is a small lane, now known as Church Lane. It leads to, and was probably once part of, a footpath known as the Almanaze Path. This unusual name appears to be either a contraction of Almen (or Almond) Hayes, by which it was known in the mid 19th century, evolving from land held by the Hayes family who lived here in the 18th century, or from the access it gave to the Elm Hays field. The field at the end of Church Lane latterly contained the October Fairs which were formerly held in the streets and, earlier still, in the churchyard.

The present vicarage was built about 1920. It stands a little to the east of the site of the earliest known vicarage which, until about 1888, stood just to the east of the church. It was widely assumed to be the last of the remaining abbey buildings. During the period between these two vicarages, the Antrobus Arms served the purpose, prior to becoming an inn. At this time also, cottages existed along what is now the vicarage wall. One was the home of the church sexton, Mr Joseph Spreadbury, during the latter part of the 19th century. Mr Spreadbury was unfortunately drowned whilst tending one of the hatches near Grey Bridge.

Examples of the varied designs on the medieval floor tiles found in 1860.

The east facade of the earliest known vicarage, as extended to accommodate the Reverend Fulwar Fowle and his family. The older portion, to the rear, was thought to be all that remained of the former priory buildings.

Across the road from the vicarage is No. 29, the former "Phoenix" cottage, now named Dunleys House. Until recently the undertaker's residence (the business having now moved a few doors down following the undertaker's retirement) it was, at the turn of the century, a temperance hostel and restaurant frequented by cyclists. On the corner of this building can be seen a niche or chamfer cut into the brickwork by an earlier occupier, a shoemaker, to permit a view up the road. Next door to the Phoenix stood the Bear Inn, referred to as a coaching inn and noted for its fine oak panelling. It was destroyed by fire in 1870. The site today houses the Dunkirk Veterans Club, the building being the former church rooms and school.

On the same side is the Antrobus Arms Hotel, formerly the Avon Temperance Hotel. The present building is much changed from the earlier Chopping Knife Inn which occupied the same site during the 18th century. The earlier character can be seen in the west wing adjoining the central hall and entrance. The blocked

Church Street from the west end, showing the former Phoenix hotel, at around the turn of the century and today.

door, formerly for horse-drawn vehicles, suggests its original purpose. The east wing is of more recent construction, being formerly an open yard. Owned at one time by the local and well-known Pinckney family, it was sold to a Reverend Meyrick who, in 1868, made extensive alterations and additions to the inn which produced the present hotel, the adjoining parish rooms and the nearby house set back from the road, called "Fairholme" - with its distinctive octagonal observatory - the whole combining to produce his residence and a school or college of noted reputation. It is recorded that teams from this school met those from Marlborough College on the Stonehenge cricket ground, reputedly the finest pitch in the county! On Sundays the scholars could be seen in their distinctive uniform of Eton jackets with silk toppers, escorted by their ushers clad in gowns and mortar-boards. It is, perhaps, a pity that Meyrick's school was so short-lived.

Church Street viewed from its eastern end at the turn of the century. Lloyds Bank now occupies the site on the left, where the gentleman stands in the doorway. The fine building across the road made way in 1970 for the present Abbey Square shopping precinct. Further down the road on the left is the King's Arms Inn, and beyond that the vicarage which was to become the present Antrobus Arms Hotel.

Opposite the Antrobus Arms were cottages and gardens in the 18th century. More recently, when the vicarage and hotel car park were constructed, skeletons were found buried as if in a cemetery; possibly one connected with the monastic house. Skeletal remains feature in the former buildings on the adjoining premises also. Where the Abbey Square now stands, with its changing selection of shops and restaurants, stood a fine 17th century red-brick house, with stone mullioned windows, leaded lights and distinctive chimney. This was, at the end of the 18th century, the residence of one Dr Bloxham who, as an aid to his medical practice, kept a complete skeleton in a cupboard, as did most GP's at that time. The house was later divided into separate dwellings and was occupied by a saddler's family who used the adjacent stable and coach house as a shop, and by the carrier who was also the postman. Around the mid 20th century the saddlery became an upholstery shop. Both of these buildings were demolished in 1971.

Opposite is the King's Arms Inn, formerly the Saracen's Head. Although a building of early character and typical of many here that have long since gone, its use as an inn does not seem to have preceded the 18th century, being referred to in 1726 as a house, orchard and paddock belonging to a Mr Hays, the premises extending almost to Frog Lane (now Flower Lane). Earlier Amesbury historians have inferred its existence as an inn in 1763, when it is recorded by John Soul that

"...the old Amesbury Friendly Society met here..." After the demise of the nearby market house, the inn was the meeting place of the courts Leet and Baron.

The eastern end of Church Street at its junction with High Street and Salisbury Street. The major area of change between 1910 and the present day is at the left of the illustrations, where the former thatched saddlery and haulier's dwelling provided, in 1970, the site for the present Abbey Square shopping precinct.

Between this building and Lloyds Bank on the corner of Church Street and Salisbury Street were shops and houses, the former exhibiting the bow window of which there now remains only one example, and this in Salisbury Street. The bank occupies approximately the site of the 18th century market house which stood in a commanding position at the north end of the market place, now Salisbury Street. The site was at the boundary of the Priory and Earldoms manors and the natural meeting place when both manors came under the one owner after the dissolution. The only surviving illustration of the market house suggests that the stocks - the machinery for punishment of local crimes - were also here, but this is not certain. It is known that they changed their location at various times. We are more certain that the public weighbridge was here, essential in later years for the assessment of tolls but even this moved to the south end of the market before it was rendered obsolete.

Having reached the market house, another convenient moment arises in which to pause and consider briefly its background and meaning to the local community as illustrated by the remaining accounts of the manorial court; for the market house was, in many ways, the focal point of communal life - it contained the weights and measures, thus governing the standard of trade, and was also while it stood, the meeting place of the manorial court.

A modern view of Church Street looking west.

Manorial Life

As we have seen earlier, Amesbury has evolved from a typical manorial system. Each class of person was kept very much in place by the manorial courts which made use of local unpaid officers. These courts - Courts Leet and Baron for Amesbury - concerned themselves with land holding and transfers, rents, fines and services, common rules for cultivation and land management and the various rights of grazing, timber, fuel etc. The duties of each person were prescribed - to do service for the lord, to fight when required and to obey the seemingly complex but necessary system·of farming and, last of all, to support himself and his family as best he could. Every action was regulated by the local court which was held in the market house every three weeks or so, and annually.

Intimate detail of life in Amesbury under its various manorial lords is scarce. All we have left now is one Book of Presentments of the Courts Leet and Baron for the Priory and Earldom Manors, which covers the period 1730 to 1854. The Court Leet concerned itself with minor infringements of the law, while the Court Baron dealt with property and other territorial transactions. This remaining book of Presentments - earlier books, thought to date from the 14th century, were consigned to fuel a fire earlier this century - just lifts a corner of the curtain, giving a glimpse of the workings and life of manorial Amesbury.

With the one book we have left we can just see the workings of the manorial courts during their final period of decline, to the point where they became a legal formality, finally giving way to the onslaught of Victorian legislation and reform. The book was purchased by fifteen of the twenty jurymen who, with the two constables, two bailiffs, hayward, wayman and other officers, were elected annually. The initial entries reflect the importance of the courts to the local community. The Presentments begin by listing the rights and customs, the origins and fuller detail of which were long since lost; authority for an action being established by it being "....according to the customs of the manor..." and as such the local tenant farmers were instructed:

The cows of ye Lord to go three days in each corne field before ye sheep.
A right for ye herd of cows of Great Amesbury to have three days feed in a little meadow called ye Butts and likewise in ye Little ffield after harvest before Mr Haywards sheep.
Earls Farm flock of sheep to have no right of feed on Cuckold Hill and Townsend Field till 9 days before Michelmas.
The Occupier of Countess Farm to have no way nor right of way to drive any manner of cattle through cowleas to lower leas from Ladyday to Martinstide...
...(has) a right way through New Leas to drive any manner of cattle to King's Island between Hollary Day and Martens Tide...
It is contrary to the customs of the manor to put any beasts into the Common before 3rd of May.
...contrary for horses to be put into the Common before Lammas.
...custom of this manor for the tennants who have a Right of Common to have a right to the shroud of trees standing thereon.
Part of the Common field is enclosed near Parsonage Lane now in the occupation of William Warne.
Occupiers of Countess Court Farm for enclosing part of the Common near Dark Lane throughing to another manor.

Having laid the ground rules to ensure that all things happened at an appointed time, the courts then had to ensure that the rules were obeyed. In this respect a certain Farmer Scanes receives particular attention:

...for allowing his ewes and lambs to feed on the Summer Field before St Georges day.
...for putting more sheep on the Common than he was supposed to...
...for putting sheep in Martins Field against custom...
...for not putting a bull to the herd of beasts according to custom...

The Market House: demolished after a fire in 1809. A suggestion of stocks is just visible at the far end.

All this and more for Farmer Scanes, at only one meeting of the court. One might be tempted to feel sorry for him, except that he does appear as one of the elected jurors whose aim should perhaps have been to uphold and practise the rules, rather than to ignore them. Not a very good example to the "ordinary man in the field"!

His attitude does, however, help to illustrate the dwindling powers of the courts and of the manorial system during this period. No fines or punishments are recorded against his misdemeanours, it was already too futile an exercise to try and impose such penalties. The growing disillusionment felt by the ordinary person is perhaps shown by the entry for 17th October 1746, which records one "...Asa Childs for breaking open the pound" - a commonly used ploy to recover one's beasts and avoid paying the fine.

It was also the business of the courts to exercise authority in respect of the maintenance of territorial boundaries, the provision of standard weights and measures and the continuing good order of the various buildings in the community, all of which were owned by the lord. Hence we see the following typical entries:

> Mr Blatch the proprietor of Ratfyn Farm has encroached on the manor by plowing half the ditch between Ratfyn and Earls farms.
> Mr Hutchins has encroached on the manor by planting fir trees over the boundary between Porton and Red House Farms.
> ...the ditch in Great Boney Meadow should be cleared by the owner...
> John Osgood for ploughing 3 feet beyond his bounds near Salisbury Way.

Farmer Coster for hedging part of the Common near Shallow Water Meadow.
Mr Poore and Mr Pinckney for not keeping up the fence about Northam according to custom.
...Farmer Blake for breaking up a Linchet in South Mill Hill Field...
The Pit at the great Elm to be very dangerous for people or cattle to fall into.
The Pound...and Stocks...to be very much out of repair which is great deniance to the benefits of the tenants and ought to be repaired by the Lord of the said Manor.
...the Duke of Queensberry for causing part of a bank called Whitnam Bank to be carried away being part of the Common.
...the bound(ary) stalks in the field to be out of repair and the tenants desire that it should be done by the Lords of this Severall Manors.
...the Quart and Pint standard which was burnt and the weights and scales to be provided by His Grace.

These last entries help to give some idea of the responsibilities to be met by the head of the community. However, the number of times that the same entries appear in the court records before the action called for was completed gives an indication of the lack of interest felt by the Duke of Queensberry towards the well-being of his town and people. The action of Asa Childs recorded above can, no doubt, be excused in the atmosphere of mounting frustration that must have existed.

Things could only improve. Eventually they did but not, apparently, until the estate came into the hands of Sir Edmund Antrobus in 1824. Among the entries during his period of ownership, it is recorded that a blindhouse was erected for the use of the town and a woodhouse was erected in Tanners Lane. A survey of the manorial boundaries was made in 1830, in the presence of Sir Edmund, after which about thirty men - presumably the jurors and other officers - dined at the New Inn. The remainder received bread, cheese and beer at the King's Arms. The entry for the following year was very brief, "...We present all things well." This brevity is characteristic of the later entries, which concern themselves with the poor state of some of the roads - South Mill Hill being dangerous for carts and carriages and the turnpike near the churchyard being very narrow and dangerous for coaches. In 1843 John Harrison, the last hayward, was "made redundant", his job being taken over by the relatively new rural police. The last notable entry appears in 1851 which says: "The footpath in Bakehouse Lane out of repair; likewise our manure heap."

High Street

Continuing eastwards into the High Street we cross Abbey Lane which once led directly from the market place into the priory grounds. In the 18th century this was lined with houses, barns and gardens. Remaining evidence of this earlier character can be seen in the portion of cob wall and the brick and timber construction at the rear of the present newsagent and hardware shop. The importance of this part of Amesbury, as reflected in its buildings of older and superior architectural style, is also evident in the adjoining house and shop, until recently a clothing and shoe shop but currently undergoing transformation following a change in ownership.

Across the road from these premises is the former gaol, lock-up or blindhouse, situated on the corner of High Street and Salisbury Street. Erected in 1827, it replaces an earlier one incorporated in the abbey gatehouse, possibly Kent House. Its present role of estate agent's office requires a little more decoration and fittings than would have been thought desirable for its original purpose, consisting as it did, of two cells, each with its heavy iron-studded door and grill. The building has not been confined to these two uses; it has been a florist's, a motorcycle shop in the 1920's and, more recently, a milk bar and restaurant. An amazing variety of uses for such small premises!

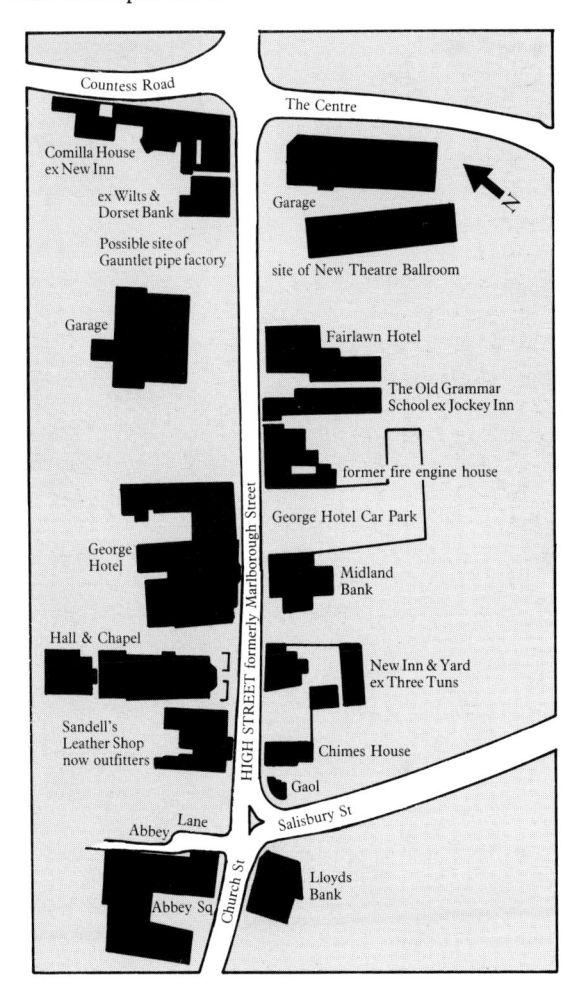

The former gaol at the corner of Salisbury Street and High Street. Later becoming a florist's, motor cycle retailer, and milk-bar, it currently offers an estate agency and financial services. What next...?

Chimes House - once housed the offices of Amesbury's electricity supply company and, in the illustration, is again seen at the centre of technological advance!

Next to the gaol, in the High Street, is a 17th or 18th century house standing now on what was given as "Church Land" in 1726. At present a hairdressing establishment, it too has seen a variety of uses. Known at one time as Chimes House, it is recorded as being left as a legacy to the church by the mechanic who invented, installed and maintained the three-hour chimes in the church. The exact period in question is uncertain. Early in the 1920's it became the offices of the Amesbury Electric Light Company and later still, up to around the mid-1950's, it was the local wireless shop.

Next to Chimes House we have the New Inn and its car park. The rough chalk-block construction typical of this area can be clearly seen in the east wall. The inn is recorded in the 18th century as the Three Tuns Inn and Garden, run by one widow Vincent. The car-park, originally a tenement garden backing on to Marlborough Street (now High Street) became, around the turn of the century, the tanyard and works of the Sandell family, who continued a trade that had existed since the 14th century. Their shop was directly opposite.

Across the road from the New Inn lies the Wesleyan Chapel. The present building, constructed in 1900, is the second on the site built to accommodate those who since the 17th century were described as Dissenters. The earlier chapel was built in 1838 and further enlarged in 1892. It was approached through a stone archway and would have been positioned behind the present chapel, the front portion of which occupies the site of a bakers' shop kept by the Misses Yarham who were noted for their lardy cakes and cooked ham.

Next to the chapel is the George Hotel. The exact age and earlier history of this establishment are not certain. It has been dated to around 1560, but is thought to have existed earlier and to have had connections with the abbey, permitting rest and refreshment to travellers, pilgrims and those on business with the abbey. The character of the present building is much changed from that of former years, being altered in the 17th century, with modernisation in about 1768, and a new west wing in the early 20th century. In the 18th century it still retained the form of the traditional inn and hostelry, little changed from medieval times; a rectangular structure, with central courtyard, approached by a curving drive leading off from the High Street - this area now being occupied by the west wing. Behind the main building were the stables, outhouses, gardens and orchards. This was the inn recorded by Dr Claver Morris in his "Diary of a West Country Physician" where, on the 5th and 6th of May 1721, he lodged whilst attending the horse fair at Stonehenge after enjoying a late breakfast of beef from the spit. In later years the George Hotel was the frequent venue for large meetings. It was here that the lord of the manor would provide the annual dinner for his tenants after the yearly rent audit; here also during the 19th century the Turnpike Trustees would occasionally meet and likewise the Board of Guardians, until moving on to their new workhouse premises. It was at one time the headquarters of the All-England Coursing Club and of the New Forest Coursing Club.

Across the road from the hotel were its gardens, now a car park and the latest site of the recently revived weekly market. Next to this stands the Midland Bank. Prior to its construction the site contained the dwellings of William Cove Kemm,

The earliest available photograph of the High Street. Taken towards the end of the 19th century it shows, on the left, Sally Yarham's cake shop and the Stonehenge Temperance Hotel where now stands the Methodist chapel built in 1900. At the time of the photograph the chapel existed to the rear of the shops and was approached through the archway.

High Street shortly after the destruction of the shops and construction of the new chapel.

High Street around 1915. The addition of primitive street lighting and the evident transition from horse-drawn to motor transport marks the beginning of much wider change.

In this view, around or shortly after the first world war, the military presence is still much in evidence, the gaol appears to have fallen out of use, electricity or telegraph poles are being erected, the west wing of the George Hotel and, across the road, the Midland Bank have been constructed.

By the 1930's the change was much advanced and a new maturity evident. The George Hotel west wing was already ivy-covered. Less attractive were the electricity supply and telegraph poles.

Even today, from the west end, the fundamental structure of the street remains more or less intact, only the embellishments change.

a brewer and publican and also a noted local historian and artist. On the east side of the car park are cottages of traditional rural character. The one nearest to the car park, occupied in the 19th century by one Walton Soper, painter and parish clerk, later became the garage for the fire engine and, more recently a local taxi-driver's establishment. It is currently a betting shop. The adjoining cottage was, until fairly recently, a greengrocer's, and is now a private residence. Across the road from these, adjoining the George Hotel, are the premises formerly occupied by the town's noted butcher and poulterer whose window display might almost defeat the efforts of his modern counterparts! Although the business ceased around the mid-20th century and the shop has since been the home of various diverse activities, it still retains some of the tile-work that provided the elegant facade during its original period of use. The cattle pens and slaughter-house associated with the business have long since disappeared or have been absorbed into alternative activities, but a meat processing business still functions to the rear of the building.

Next to these premises now stands a line of shops and a bank where formerly stood houses and gardens; then comes one of the two earliest garages in Amesbury. This is also the site of Asa Childs' residence, who we saw earlier had his own ideas of local justice when his animals were impounded! It is thought that the garage site, or the immediate vicinity, was the location of the Gauntlet pipe factory, from the number of bowls and stems that have been recovered here from time to time.

Displays such as in this High Street shop between the wars are now a rarity.

Opposite the Amesbury Motor Company, formerly Sloans Garage, is the former Rose's Charity Grammar School. It is of superior traditional construction, with neatly squared and laid chalk blocks, contrasting with the less elegant construction with the same medium in adjacent buildings. This school, of 17th or 18th century origin, has seen a variety of uses. In 1726 it appears as the White Hart Inn and Gardens of Anthony Cook Kenton. Later that century it had become the Jockey Inn, with stables; it was the subject of a fire in 1751. In 1807 it became a schoolmaster's residence and grammar school, fulfilling as well the function of post office during the latter part of the 19th century. Its function as a school ceased in 1899 since when it has been a private residence. Features from its school period still exist, notably the dual-seater earth closet in the garden!

Next door is the Fairlawn Hotel. Built around the middle of the 19th century as Fovant House, the residence of Mr George Best Batho, a surgeon, it formerly included a coach-house, stables and a yard. There were two adjoining premises, the first - again with stables, coach-house and gardens - was known as Fair Lawn and was occupied during the 19th century by a Doctor Charles Pyle who, in addition to his medical practice, seems to have run some sort of finishing school for young ladies. The other building was a cottage, entered via two stone steps and was the sweet-shop of widow Eyres. Part of these premises were, more recently, a cafe which retained the Fairlawn name. They have subsequently been antique, audio and charity shops, at present housing a domestic electrical appliance shop.

The remainder of this side of the High Street to the junction with the A345 contains now a garage premises of interesting and characteristic 1930's architectural style, with recent additions. This frontage onto the High Street was formerly occupied by Robinson's the chemist and William Hough, a noted watch and clock maker who would - as was the custom then - sit in the window at his bench so that passers-by could see him at work and maybe their own watch or clock in pieces! Until the late 1950's the site also contained the New Theatre Ballroom, billed as the largest dance hall in the south-west. It featured groups, bands and many celebrity names, providing entertainment for local people over a wide area and for the troops from the nearby camps on Salisbury Plain. This corner was also the former site of Underwood's Builder's business and family home, its main frontage being onto School Lane. G W Underwood was the builder of many of the Edwardian period red-brick buildings around Salisbury Street, Flower Lane and in Edwards Road. There were usually several farm carts awaiting repair, the firm being also a carpenter's shop and wheelwright.

On the opposite side of the road is one of Amesbury's older and more interesting buildings which has seen a variety of uses. Currently under the same ownership as Comilla House it houses an antique shop and an undertaker's business. Adjoining premises, in imitation architectural style, at present a charity bric-a-brac shop, started life as a coach-house and later fulfilled the function of Wilts and Dorset Bank. However, it is the building on the corner that merits closer inspection.

Examination of the outside reveals some interesting characteristics. The stone

Until fairly recently the post office, and in earlier times the New Inn, these premises now fulfil a number of uses.

High Street from its easterly end. The building in the right foreground is now an antique shop, whilst that of the undertaker on the left of the picture is now a garage forecourt.

High Street viewed from the east end today. Character is giving way to commerce.

blocks forming the chequer work contain some of green sandstone, a material foreign to this area. It is unlikely that this would have been used from choice, unless available from a local source. It is probable therefore that this greenstone came from the demolished abbey buildings as such material was included among that sold to local people. Further possible evidence of this source of building material can be seen in the fragments of carved stonework visible on the High Street side. The corbel just under the eaves at the corner of the building, whilst also from the abbey, was placed in its present position some years ago by Len Buckland, the then owner of the building. Len, who was a veteran historian and champion of rights-of-way in the parish called it "St Michael of Amesbury". In 1726 this establishment, with the adjoining Comilla House just around the corner, is given as the New Inn, house and gardens of William Stallard. It appears likely that the house fulfilled much the same function from the early 17th century as, in the Lenten Recognisances, one Agnes Matravers, tippler, agreed not to permit meat to be prepared or sold in her house during Lent, or on any Friday. She is also given as the occupier of the house at the north-east corner of the High Street in the manorial perambulation of 1639. The premises may have been operating as an inn as late as 1829. It was certainly remembered as such in that year when William Wiltshire the butcher was killed when his cart overturned after hitting the wall of this building "at great speed". This location was evidently even then an accident black spot, as William Wiltshire was not the only person to meet his doom there, a man called Hicks meeting a similar fate a few years before.

Accidents continued to occur here until traffic lights were installed in the 1950's. The lights were removed in 1969 when the A303 by-pass was constructed, but were replaced following public demand.

The Centre

Turning right at the east end of the High Street one arrives at the Centre, which replaces the earlier School Lane or Back Lane. On the west side, close to the junction with High Street, were 18th century houses. Later, into the early 1900's, a timber yard, or pimp yard, existed on the corner, with carpenter's shop, saw-pits and a pile of huge tree trunks for cutting into timber and planks. The timber store, a most unusual building with its upper and lower sawyers pit, was nicknamed "the Ark". This area later became a taxi stand. A little further along, still within the present garage premises, a house and farm buildings were destroyed by fire in 1809, being replaced at a later date by a grain mill and store. This site eventually became a County Council depot until around the 1950's ending up, as at present, a garage yard. In the last few years a printing company has taken up residence in the yard as well. When Underwood's building business ceased in 1912 the yard became a garage for an early motor company, Jennings and Kent, which supplied and operated fairground equipment from the premises. This firm later used the site of the old National School (now the Friar Tuck Cafe) in Salisbury Street.

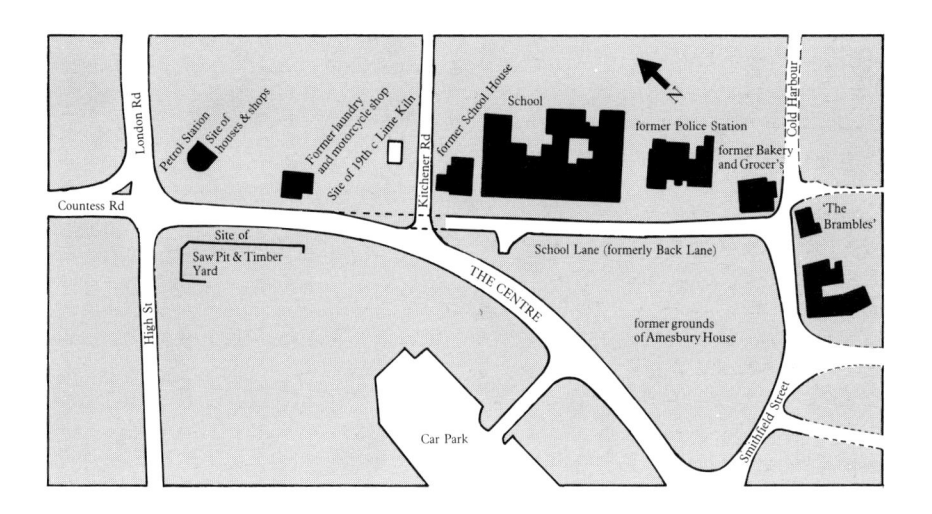

The junction of High Street, London Road, Countess Road and the Centre, as it appears today. Comilla House with its former stables and doctor's surgery, is in the right foreground.

A similar view, taken from the crossroads around 1910. Frank Tucker's drapers shop at the left has now become a petrol station, whilst the timber yard and grain store at the right are now a car sales forecourt.

The same junction in 1939. Frank Tucker's shop had become Bugdens Motor Cycle Depot before being finally demolished in the early 1940's.

A view of the same junction looking north. Countess Road leads away to the left and the trees of Lords Walk are in the background. The thatched cottages were demolished to make way for YMCA premises which, in turn, have made way for retirement dwellings.

A view along present-day School Lane, formerly Back Lane.

Opposite the present garage premises, where another petrol station flourishes today, stood a draper's shop and dwelling owned, at the turn of the century, by Frank (Dan) Tucker, the first Chairman of the Amesbury Parish Council when formed in 1894. When his business moved to Salisbury Street the premises became one of the varied sites of a motorcycle shop. By the second world war period the buildings had been demolished, the area being just waste ground and waiting for the next development.

Proceeding southwards along the Centre towards Kitchener Road, one passes the former laundry premises, later used by the electricity board and the present motorcycle shop, the latter having now moved next door, and is currently being put to use as financial advice and motor spares businesses. Next to this, the private house occupies the site of the 19th century lime kiln. Kitchener Road is of relatively recent origin and was presumably named for the usual patriotic reasons and the fact that the presence of the Army had made such a difference to the town economy. Its line corresponds with an 18th century boundary between two holdings in Town's End Little Field and it has only really evolved during this century from a trackway in the 1940's leading to a pig farm and Crooked Covert Copse. By the 1950's it was a site for mobile homes and other temporary forms of accommodation, eventually developing into an access for the present estate.

After Kitchener Road we have the former school house, school and former police station all built along the edge of the same field. Although now possessing various architectural additions and subtractions, this group of buildings still shows the attempt to produce an example of co-ordinated civic construction of the

Edwardian era. The school, built in 1901, brought together the earlier diverse charity and private educational establishments under the control of the parish church. This police station, which later became the divisional headquarters, allowed for the more efficient operation of the county police, which had been formed in 1839. It replaced the earlier police station, now demolished, which had been sited in Salisbury Street, and its associated lock-up. At the south end of School Lane is the entrance to Coldharbour. Facing the end of the lane is one of the three remaining thatched roofs which, with the house on the opposite corner, permit an impression of the earlier character that existed among these modern dwellings.

Smithfield Street

Turning right from School Lane one enters Smithfield Street. Its name may imply former use as a cattle market or fair place. This is substantiated by a recorded memory that Smithfield Street and Bakehouse Lane were remembered as being full of horses and cattle at an annual fair. Such an event would have been served by the 18th century Greyhound Inn, referred to by this name as long ago as 1740 when it was observed by the manorial court to be out of repair. The street name was reintroduced fairly recently when the health centre and library complex were built opposite the Greyhound, on the former site of Amesbury House, an early 19th century dwelling in which the Antrobus family are supposed to have resided when first coming to the town.

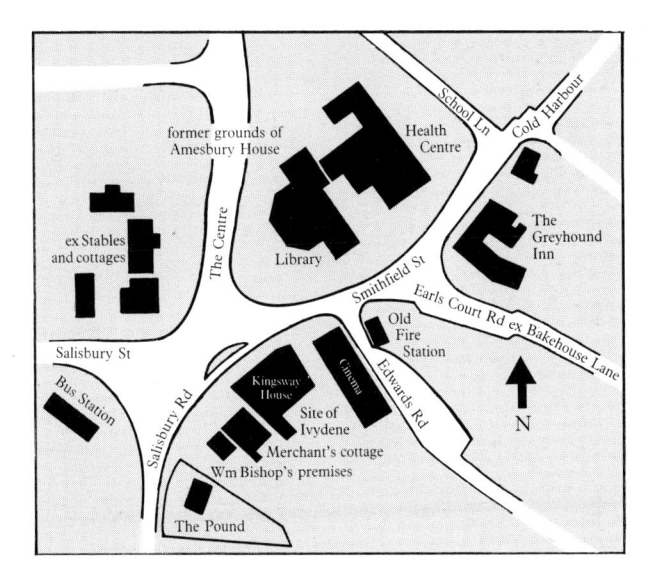

Smithfield Street and the entrance to Coldharbour just after 1900. The Greyhound Inn appears at the extreme right.

A similar view today.

138

Crossing Earls Court Road, formerly Bakers or Bakehouse Lane, one finds, situated at the north end of the 'arcade' of shops, the premises built early this century to house the town's fire engine, now replaced by the more effective establishment in Salisbury Road. This former 'fire station' has subsequently fulfilled various uses, more recently Amesbury's first library premises, a baker's and, at present, a cycle shop. At the other side of the adjacent Edwards Road, so named to remind us of Job Edwards, one of Amesbury's noted earlier historians, is the cinema. The background to this currently threatened amenity is worth considering in a little more detail.

Amesbury's Plaza Cinema, currently threatened with demolition and re-development of the site.

The cinema was sited temporarily in Salisbury Street, pending construction of the Plaza.

The Ivydene guest house was a prominent feature of the town central area. The remaining patch of grass was once a larger green.

Immediately after the burning of Ivydene in 1911 the first permanent cinema appeared. Here, the ruins of Ivydene are hidden by the cinema hoardings behind the war memorial. The cinema itself is just to the left. In the centre is the young chestnut tree planted to commemorate the coronation of George V.

The present character of the central area was becoming established in the 1930's with the arrival of the Co-operative store on the Ivydene site.

The chestnut tree, now well on its way to maturity, hides the Co-op and the newly erected Plaza cinema in this late 1930's scene. To the right, the forecourt of the Wilts and Dorset bus station replaces the cob wall visible in earlier pictures.

The central area today. War memorial, chestnut tree and green have all gone, replaced by a complex and unsightly array of telephone kiosks, road signs and markings.

Amesbury House, viewed here from the north, was demolished in the late 1960's, to make way for the library and health centre.

The cinema is situated on part of the site of the former Ivydene guest-house which was burned down in 1911. No sooner had this disaster occurred than the site became occupied by the travelling bioscope. It arrived pulled by an enormous steam tractor called "Pride of the South" and took the form of three large trailers which, when unpacked became stage, screen and projection area, the whole being assembled and contained under canvas. Owned by the now famous Chipperfield family, which lived for a time in Edwards Road, the "big top" stood more or less where the present cinema stands. With dancers and organ to provide supplementary attractions the bioscope must have made a major impact upon this still close-knit little community, attracting even those from Salisbury, whose similar cinematographic establishments it is thought to have preceded. The canvas top was eventually succeeded by a more permanent wooden building which after a while itself proved unsuitable to cope with the large audiences that were attracted to the shows. The cinema was then moved temporarily to the present site of Logan's DIY store next to the bus station. In 1936 the magnificent modern edifice was constructed and opened by Miss Betty Fields, Gracie's sister. The new cinema however, even with its modern brick construction in art-deco style and improved comfort lacked the air of rural informality of its forerunner. The occasional collapse of a row of seats in later years was no match for the days of silent films when the delight of the audience was not solely confined to the actions displayed on the screen but also included close attention to the manual dexterity of the person operating the sound effects and showing ribald appreciation when those effects failed to coincide with the actions they were meant to help illustrate.

Returning to the pre-cinema era, Ivydene was a thatched guesthouse with adjacent malthouse containing wooden lattice windows, which was approached via massive gates with pillars. It was, in the 19th century, the residence of Job Edwards, the local maltster and antiquarian. Its destruction by fire was a fate met by so many of the town's buildings; the fire removing what was probably a building of major importance to the character of central Amesbury, allowing, once it had gone, the beginning of a new wave of architectural development. The Ivydene fire was undoubtedly the first great test of the 22-man manual fire engine purchased by the Amesbury Fire Brigade Committee as one of its first actions when formed in 1902. If people have a mind to complain about today's fire service, let them think how the owners of Ivydene must have felt, waiting with bucket in hand whilst horses were rounded up in the field at the bottom of Coldharbour, led to the engine-house in the High Street and harnessed up to eventually rush to the scene. Providing there was sufficient hose to reach the river and enough strong men, the action could then commence! The distance from the river proved problematical in the Ivydene case, requiring the additional assistance of the Salisbury fire brigade, the Artillery brigade from Bulford and help from the employees of the Bristol Aeroplane Company at Larkhill. Such was the gravity of these occasions that the help of everyone was welcomed; passers-by, hotel residents, locals and the vicar. It was also noted in contemporary accounts that certain idle local persons would not assist in manning the engine but were happy to just stand by and watch the action!

The last remaining evidence of Ivydene and its owner was a little summerhouse positioned in the corner of the yard behind Kingsway House - the former Co-operative store, currently housing a sports shop, delicatessen, greengrocer and fitness centre. The summerhouse was built with more of the surplus material from the 1853 church restoration. It came to light again in 1956 during extension work on the Co-op, when undergrowth and creepers that were hiding it were removed. The summerhouse was demolished in the early 1970's and it is believed that the materials have been stored by the CRS until it can be decided where to re-erect it. It is to be hoped that a decision can be reached soon before another link with Amesbury's history is lost. At the time of writing it is understood that negotiations are still slowly proceeding, to establish the location of the carefully numbered stones.

The house immediately to the right, known earlier as Merchant's cottage and currently the dentist's surgery, was one of the sites of the nomadic post office which moved here during the latter part of the 19th century from "Ye Olde Shoppe" (the bakery) in Salisbury Street. References to the Merchant family occur in the 1639 perambulation. Adjoining this building are the former business premises and timber yard of William Bishop, the local builder, undertaker, mason and general handyman, around the turn of the century. This family is also well established in the history of the town, earlier members being elected jurors to the manorial court in the 18th and 19th centuries.

Bishop's timber yard abutted onto another of the few but important former public facilities, the pound. Its purpose was to contain such livestock that had strayed, caused damage or were not readily identifiable, until the owner could be traced and made to pay the fine incurred for whatever damage or inconvenience was involved. The original structure is, of course, no longer visible but the name lives on with the present house on the site. Opposite the pound were cob-walled cottages where now a modern brick wall still stands feebly attempting to hide huge lorries.

Flower Lane

Continuing westwards past the pound we reach the junction of Salisbury Road and Flower Lane, this portion of the lane being formerly called Tanners Lane, presumably a reminder of a craft that was practised here prior to the 18th century, or the surname of a forgotten family. On the north side of the entrance the three cottages, although having long-since lost their thatched roofs, again remind one of the older character of the area. Here also was the blacksmith's premises; a person who had to be a master of his craft to keep a community going. On the south side of the entrance, the pet shop - formerly a seed merchant's premises - replaces an earlier wheelwright's establishment. An extremely large lime tree, which was either blown down or struck by lightning in the early part of the century, is remembered in the name of one of the cottages. Whilst here, we can also spend a minute considering the fire station and the service that has been provided over the

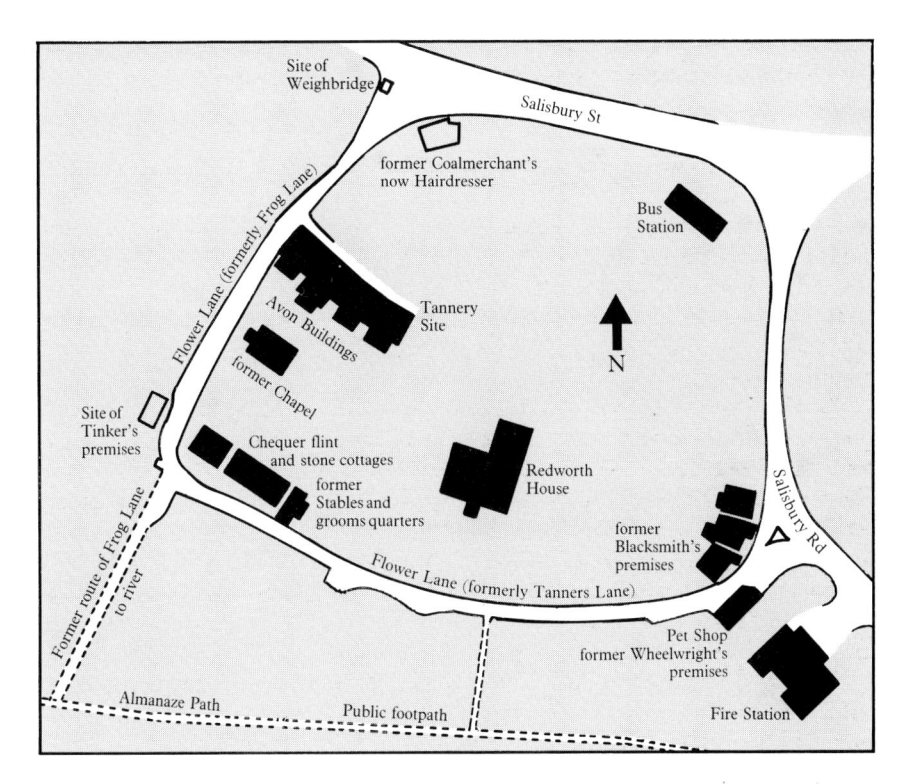

The fall of Bishop's lime tree in Flower Lane. Occasions like this were always guaranteed to draw a crowd.

The first motorised fire engine, a Daimler, acquired around 1920.

The second fire engine, a Dennis, and its brigade, just before the second world war.

years. As we saw earlier, the Fire Brigade Committee was formed at the beginning of this century and acquired a manual engine. Prior to this, the only equipment available to fight the fires was the engine invented by Reverend Thomas Holland and such ladders and hooks that might be available to pull thatch from burning roofs. Hence, the acquisition of the manual engine used at Ivydene was a considerable advantage except that it seems to have depended on being in reasonable proximity to the river. Another major step forward occurred a little later, possibly around 1920, with the arrival of a motorised engine. Housed in its new garage next to the cinema, its presence helped the townspeople to sleep much more soundly in their beds! In 1938 responsibility for the fire brigade passed to the Rural District Council and in 1942 the fire service became nationalised. In 1947 it came under the influence of the Fire Services Act and from that time has been run by the County Council as fire authority. The present accommodation for the now much enlarged fire brigade was constructed in the early 1960's.

Continuing on round Flower Lane one arrives at Redworth House. This 19th century building was the residence of a prosperous builder called Quint Cole. It later became the meeting place of the Amesbury Rural District Council and is now used principally by the Social Services Department of the County Council, and the Salisbury District Council, part of the duties being the tourist information office. The town manure heap, referred to earlier, was also here at the corner of the grounds! Passing hastily on, one reaches a cottage abutting onto the lane, the former stables and groom's quarters. Next to this is a row of attractive early 19th century cottages in chequer flint and stone. The first of these, Vine Cottage, was, at the beginning of this century, the residence of one Edward Randall, a noted glove and breeches maker, whose additional responsibilities as verger extended to ringing the "death bell" at the passing of his fellow townspeople. He also, apparently, assumed the rights to the proceeds from the orchard behind the cottages and it wasn't until after his death that it was realised he had been pocketing the income without authority! The cottages are situated at the former junction of Tanners Lane and Frog Lane, the latter being the part that ran east-west from the river up to Salisbury Street.

Turning the corner into "Frog Lane" there was, at the beginning of this century, a tinker's premises where now exists the entrance to the British Telecom exchange. Across the way is a former Primitive Methodist chapel, constructed from corrugated iron sheet and painted green. No-one is quite sure when it was last used as a chapel or by what denomination but general opinion has suggested that it fulfilled its original purpose until the early part of this century, being used by a handful of people up to the outbreak of the first world war. At that time it had no minister and services were conducted by a lay preacher, a shepherd named Cooper who lived in Mill Lane. From here up to Salisbury Street the character of Flower Lane has altered appreciably. At one time the whole of the western side consisted of thatched cottages, but gradually they all went and were replaced by red-brick cottages and terraces most of which, in turn, went in the 1950's. Those remaining give some idea of the former character. Avon Buildings, for instance, are on the site of the former tanyards according to local tradition. This may account for the wool warehouse or store that existed in front of Avon Buildings at the turn of the century. It was replaced by dwellings and shops which, in turn, were demolished about twenty years ago, the site remaining vacant for some time and used for a car park and market site until redeveloped into the present row of shops. The hairdresser's establishment at the south corner of Flower Lane and Salisbury Street replaces an earlier thatched dwelling and coal merchant's premises. On the opposite side the public weighbridge was sited during the early years of this century until becoming obsolete, the facility being removed to the east end of the town. Here also one could have seen another product of local talent, one Joe "Boneser" the contortionist, more familiarly known as "Dick-a-Dick". He lived in a rough shed made from sheet iron and sacking, along the Wittenham path, near to the tollhouse in Stonehenge Road, but his "pitch" was at the end of Flower Lane, where he would delight youngsters with exhibitions of his skill in fire-eating and glass-eating. And so, by a devious route, we find ourselves in Salisbury Street.

Salisbury Street

If the north end of Salisbury Street, with its market house, manorial court and close proximity to the abbey was the civic and religious focal point of the town, then the southern end achieved a balance by its equally important commercial activities of trade and the cattle and horse fairs, bringing together the people from outlying villages to the south and east over the downs along Edmiston Road, Allington Road, Newton Toney Road, the Durnford Path and West Amesbury Wood-Way, all of which, in the 18th century, converged on Bakehouse Lane and South Mill Lane and from these on to the Market Place, now Salisbury Street.

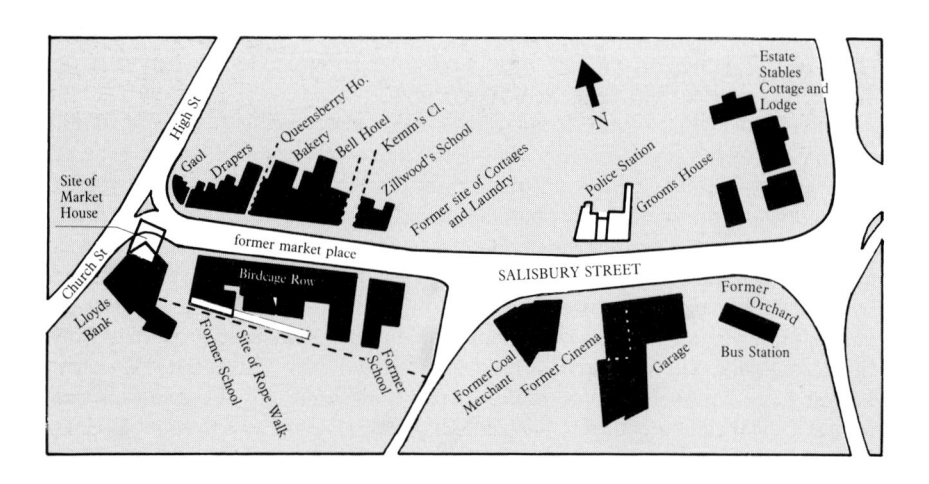

Salisbury Street viewed from its north-west end at the time of the first world war.

A similar view today.

The earliest impression we can gain of the street, or market place, is from the beginning of the 18th century at which time its character was totally different from that of today. It possessed all the traditional character expected of such an important part of the town. The street was twice the width of the present road, with large mature trees along its centre. It was bounded on the west with orchards and gardens and a rope-walk where now exists "Birdcage Row", with its various shops and services. Built in the 19th century as a row of estate cottages with schools at each end, they effectively halved the width of the market place, probably helping in its decline. The school at the southern end was the National Infants School, the older children attending the other one at the north end of the row. This latter establishment later became a garage during the early part of this

The junction of Salisbury Street and Flower Lane in the late 19th century. The entrance to Flower Lane is in the centre of the picture. The buildings on the right form part of "Birdcage Row".

The junction today. The thatched cottages have given way to more commercial premises.

The south-east end of the street. The picturesque cottages were demolished to make way for a garage premises which was subsequently demolished for a supermarket development.

century, followed by use as a grocery and currently as a cafe. An idea of the former line of the west side of the market can be gained by the position of the house - now offices - between the cafe and bank.

The east side of the market was built up with houses, closes and the hostelry very necessary for the proper conduct of market affairs but today a great deal of this earlier character has been lost. Mid-way along the east side of the street, the present Bell Inn, built in 1908, replaces an earlier hostelry of the same name, which was recorded as existing in 1880. This in turn was apparently constructed on the site of a collapsed residence in the tenancy of one Philpot, which may have been the Swan Inn, noted in the mid-18th century as being handy for the market, and known to have existed during the 17th century. Next to the Bell, and opposite the former infants school, was another 19th century educational establishment run by the Zillwood family; it is currently an estate agent's premises. The north end still retains a semblance of its former self in spite of the recent "tidying up" of some of the facade which, although done sympathetically and with the best of intention still manages to increasingly distance the present character from the earlier. However, the buildings are still a pleasing group of bakery, solicitor's (formerly the Queensberry Hotel) and draper's. The bakery is thought to date from the 16th or early 17th century and contains a chimney stack with an early 17th century carved overmantle and additional panelling.

During the first quarter of this century an alleyway called Kemm's Square led along the side of the present Bell Inn to private dwellings. Other similar alleys existed, one approximately opposite Flower Lane and another next to Ye Olde Shoppe bakery. This one has at some time in the past been infilled to form more commercial premises. It was last used as an hairdressing establishment but has been unoccupied for some years.

Considerable development has occurred at the southern end of the street, each property offering its own architect's translation of earlier styles into the contemporary scene but the area still contains inferior utilitarian architecture, with bus station, garages and home improvement centre. One redeeming feature is the former gate-house and stables of the now vanished Amesbury House. These 19th century buildings lay derelict for some time and were in danger of demolition but have been successfully developed and restored to become an attractive central town house and office site, the cottage possessing the last hand water pump in the town.

The junction of Salisbury Street and Salisbury Road showing the former bus garage area which has been under consideration for redevelopment.

In Conclusion

From what we have seen on this survey it is clear that the town has experienced an intensive period of change over the last hundred years. Not all of the change has been for the general good and most has been for commercial gain, the result of which has left some permanent scars, sweeping away traditional buildings that have stood the test of time and which have helped to form the town's distinctive character over many centuries. For example, from once exhibiting a predominance of thatched roofs, the town now has only three remaining. Traditional buildings have been replaced with purpose-built architecture, the least requirement of some of it being that it should blend harmoniously with its surroundings. There is, more recently, a detectable movement which suggests that the inhabitants and local authorities are once again taking more than just a passing interest in the character of the town. The threat today seems to come from government policies and nationally based companies always eager for new developments. Amesbury is currently poised with major new developments proposed for the central, southern and eastern areas; developments which will significantly alter its progress and propel it into taking on a markedly different role. Let us hope that vision, where it counts, can still capture and retain such traditional character that remains and blend with it the new to recreate a focus, before it is too late.

NOTES

1 General sources for this section, Richards, 1985; RCHM, 1979; Wiltshire County Council Sites and Monuments Record.
2 Richards, 1985, 15
3 RCHM, 1979, 20-2
4 Hunter-Mann, 1988
5 Branigan, 1973
6 eg. Wacher, 1978, 129-30
7 Cunnington, 1930, 172-3, 186
8 Hunter-Mann, 1988
9 Morris, 1973, 100; Myres, 1986, 160-1, 212-13
10 Gover, et al. 1939, 358-9
11 Hunter-Mann, 1988
12 Kemm, 1970, 8; since this reference was noted in the first edition of this book it has also been taken up by Bonney, 1983
13 Ball, 1979, 41
14 Robinson, 1984
15 Gover, et al. 1939, xiv, 359; but not considered by Gelling, 1978, 158-61
16 Hinton, 1979, 24
17 Pugh, 1947, 101-2
18 Jones, 1961, 229-31
19 Hinton, 1979, 27-8
20 Haslam, 1984, 129-32
21 General sources for this chapter, Hinton, 1979; Pugh, 1956
22 Wherwell may have been a refoundation, Farmer, 1979, 48
23 Stafford, 1978, 24
24 Chandler, 1978; Diverres, 1979; Diverres, 1984
25 Rollason, 1978, 68; Diverres, 1984
26 Alternative interpretations, Hinton, 1979, 25-7; RCHM, 1987, 234-5
27 Chandler, 1987, 12
28 RCHM, 1987, 234
29 Brown and Colvin, 1963, 88-90
30 Knowles, 1940, 362
31 General sources for this section, Chettle, 1942; Pugh, 1956
32 Knowles, 1940, 204
33 Kirby, 1956, 166
34 RCHM, 1987, 235
35 *Devizes Gazette*, 3.8.1899 (WANHS Library, Cuttings, 7,231)
36 Since 1979, when this account was first published, a more detailed investigation has been made which reaches the same general conclusions but adds significant further evidence, RCHM, 1987, 233-5.
37 General source for this section, Chandler, 1978
38 Pugh, 1947, no.100
39 Pugh, 1947, no.15; Pugh, 1978, no.788
40 For this paragraph see Pugh, 1947-8
41 Pugh, 1947, no.32
42 Pugh, 1947, no.75
43 Pugh, 1947, no.8
44 Grant 20.12.1252 (*Charter Rolls*, vol.1, 1903, 413); 1268/9 (*Report of Royal Commission on Market Rights and Tolls*, vol.1 (HC.1888,liii), 119, but not calendared in Charter Rolls, vol.2); 11.4.1317 (*Charter Rolls, vol.3, 1908, 333*). *Kemm, 1970, 1 reports a grant in 1219, but of this there is no trace; a grant in 1226/7 recorded in RCMRT* is a misreading for Ramsbury, see Hardy, T.D. *Rotuli litterarum clausarum*, vol.2, 1844, 174.
45 Pugh, 1947, no.96
46 Pugh, 1947, no.67; Chandler, 1985, no.844

47 Pugh, 1947, nos.9,15,63
48 Edwards, 1876, 48
49 Pugh, 1947, no.67
50 Figures in this paragraph are from Beresford, 1959
51 General sources for this section, Youings, 1972; Pugh, 1956, 254-7
52 General sources for this section, Edwards, 1876; Moore, 1976; Bold, 1988
53 Batey, 1988, 79; Bold, 1988, 120
54 Blyth, 1967, 163; Bold, 1988, 97, 110
55 Britton, 1801, 152-3
56 General sources for this section, 1851 census enumerators' returns for Amesbury; Kemm, 1970; WRO: Amesbury tithe award; trade directories
57 Ruddle, 1901, 537, shows an adult population in 1676 of 850, which probably reflects a total population of 1,200-1,400
58 WRO 944/1
59 Pugh, 1947, no.78
60 Pugh, 1947, nos.130,151; WRO 283/6
61 WRO 944/3
62 WRO 283/202
63 WRO: Amesbury tithe award
64 Kemm, 1970, 6
65 Hobsbawm and Rudé, 1973, 94; Kemm, 1970, 7
66 Bettey, 1977, 25-9
67 Britton, 1801, 153
68 Cobbett, 1958, 313-4, 318
69 General sources for Amesbury pipes, Brown, 1959; Atkinson, 1965, 1970, 1972; Stevens, 1882
70 An account of this family has recently been published, Shute, 1986, 200-6
71 Aubrey, 1847, 35; Fuller, 1952, 604
72 Ruddle, 1893-5
73 General source for this section, Chandler, 1979
74 Hardy, 1906, 169; Noyes, 1913, 248
75 General sources for this section, Kemm, 1970; trade directories
76 Documentary evidence for a Stonehenge fair is elusive, but Goulstone, 1985, 83 notes that in 1781 racing and other sports were being held at Stonehenge at "old" midsummer, 4th-5th July. The retention of old-style dating implies that the custom was older than 1752. See also Chippindale, 1983, 43
77 WRO 377/4, letter 5.3.1792
78 General source for the workhouse, Goodhugh, 1970; see also chapter 8 below
79 Kemm, 1970, 4; WANHS Library, Cuttings 7,224; 14,222
80 Kemm, 1970, 3-4; WANHS Library, Cuttings 7,224
81 Kemm, 1970, 5; WANHS Library, Cuttings 7,224
82 (both 1899 fires): WANHS Library, Cuttings 7,376; 12,54; 14,222
83 Kemm, 1970, 9; WANHS Library, Cuttings 7,224
84 WANHS Library, Cuttings 13,128
85 Willoughby, 1971
86 Thorpe, 1979, 228
87 WRO D1/54/1
88 Ransome, 1972, 24
89 WRO D1/56/7
90 WRO D1/56/9
91 Willoughby, 1971
92 A collection of Fowle's sermons is in Salisbury Local Studies Library
93 Reeves, 1956, 112-13
94 Webb, 1890-3, 41; WRO D1/54/10; Chandler, 1985, no.A15
95 Turner, 1911; John Evans list of dissenting congregations 1715-29 (in Dr Williams's Library, Gordon Square, London); Chandler, 1985, no.226
96 Wesley, 1909

97 Chandler, 1985, *passim*
98 WRO D1/56/8
99 Kemm, 1970, 2
100 General sources for schools, Kemm, 1970; *Endowed charities (County of Wilts) return*, parish of Amesbury (1905); WRO 1315/1; trade directories
101 General sources for the army, James, 1987; Parker, 1977; Clarke-Smith, 1975
102 General sources for railways, Moon, 1977; Thody, 1974

Bibliography

This bibliography includes the principal published sources for the history of Amesbury (excluding Stonehenge and Boscombe Down), as well as a number of more general works which have been used in the preparation of this book. Abbreviations are as follows: VCH = *Victoria History of the Counties of England: Wiltshire;* WAM = *Wiltshire Archaeological and Natural History Magazine;* WNQ = *Wiltshire Notes and Queries.*

Amesbury district plan: report of studies, 1975, Salisbury District Council

Amesbury Society, 1985, *In and around Amesbury*, Amesbury Society

Antrobus, F C M, 1908, *A sentimental and practical guide to Amesbury and Stonehenge*, revised edition [ca.1908], Amesbury Estate Office

Atkinson, D R, 1965, 'Clay tobacco pipes and pipemakers of Marlborough', in *WAM*, vol.60, 85-96

Atkinson, D R, 1970, 'Clay tobacco pipes and pipemakers of Salisbury, Wiltshire', in *WAM*, vol.65, 177-89

Atkinson, D R, 1972, 'Further notes on clay tobacco pipes and pipemakers from the Marlborough and Salisbury districts', in *WAM*, vol.67, 149-56

Atkinson, R J C, 1956, *Stonehenge*, Hamish Hamilton

Aubrey, J, 1847, *The natural history of Wiltshire...*, Wiltshire Topographical Society

Backinsell, W G C, 1979, *The medieval clock in Amesbury Abbey*, South Wiltshire Industrial Archaeology Society

Bagley, J J and A J, 1966, *The English poor law*, Macmillan

Ball, P F, 1979, 'The Saxon crosses at Amesbury', in Chandler, 1979b, 32-46

Barlow, F, 1970, *Edward the Confessor*, Eyre and Spottiswoode

Batey, M, 1988, 'Practical poetry: the landscaping of Amesbury Abbey', in *Country Life*, 4.2.1988, 78-80

Beresford, M W, 1959, 'Fifteenths and tenths: quotas of 1334', and 'Poll-tax payers in 1377', in *VCH Wilts*, vol.4, 294-313

Bettey, J H, 1977, *Rural life in Wessex, 1500-1900*, Moonraker Press

Bettey, J H, 1979, 'Farming and community life in Amesbury and district during the 16th and 17th centuries', in Chandler, 1979b, 58-69

Birch, S. 1788-9, *The abbey of Ambresbury: a poem*, 2 parts, T.Cadell et al

Blyth, H, 1967, *Old Q, the rake of Piccadilly: a biography of the 4th duke of Queensberry*, Weidenfeld and Nicolson

Bold, J, 1988, *Wilton House and English Palladianism: some Wiltshire houses*, HMSO (RCHME)

Bonney, D J, 1983, 'Pagan Saxon burials at Amesbury', in *WAM*, vol.77, 150

Brakspear, H, 1899-1901, 'On the Jessye at Amesbury', in *WNQ*, vol.3, 366-8

Branigan, K, 1973, 'Vespasian in the south-west', in *Proceedings of the Dorset Natural History and Archaeological Society*, vol.95, 50-7

Britton, J, 1801, *The beauties of Wiltshire*, vol.2, Vernor and Hood

156

Brown, R A, and Colvin, H M, 1963, 'The Angevin kings 1154-1216', in Brown, R A, et al (ed.) *The history of the king's works*, vol.1, HMSO, 19-50

Brown, W E, 1959, 'Tobacco and clay pipes', in *VCH Wilts*, vol.4, 240-4

Chandler, J H, 1978, 'Three Amesbury legends', in *Hatcher Review*, no.6, 12-23

Chandler, J H, 1979a, *The Amesbury Turnpike Trust*, South Wiltshire Industrial Archaeology Society

Chandler, J H, (ed.) 1979b, *The Amesbury millennium lectures*, Amesbury Society

Chandler, J H, (ed.) 1985, *Wiltshire dissenters' meeting house certificates and registrations, 1689-1852*, Wiltshire Record Society (40)

Chandler, J H, 1987, *Salisbury and its neighbours*, Salisbury Civic Society

Chettle, H F, 1942, 'The English houses of the order of Fontevraud', in *Downside Review*, no.70, 33-55

Chippindale, C, 1983, *Stonehenge complete*, Thames and Hudson

Clarke-Smith, E, 1975, 'Salisbury Plain', in *The Tidworth guide: an information handbook and directory*, 65-85

Clifford, H D, 1960, 'Where medieval nuns resided', in *Country Life*, vol.128 (1.9.1960), 442-3

Cobbett, W, 1958, *Rural rides*, Macdonald

Cunliffe, B W, 1978, *Iron age communities in Britain*, 2nd ed, Routledge and Kegan Paul

Cunnington, M E, 1930, 'Romano-British Wiltshire...', in *WAM*, vol.45, 166-216

Darlington, R R, 1955, 'Translation of the text of the Wiltshire Domesday', in *VCH Wilts*, vol.2, 113-68

Department of the Environment, 1988, *Thirty-eighth list of buildings of special architectural or historic interest...District of Salisbury (Wiltshire)...*, Department of the Environment

Diverres, A H, 1979, 'Saint Melor: what is the truth behind the legend?' in Chandler, 1979b, 9-19

Diverres, A H, 1984, 'The life of Saint Melor', in *Medieval French textual studies in memory of T B W Reid*, (Anglo-Norman Text Society occasional publications series, 1), 41-53

Dufty, A R, 1947, 'Amesbury Church', *Archaeological Journal*, vol.104, 156-8

Edwards, J, 1876, *Amesbury gleanings: chiefly in reference to the association of the families of Seymour and Douglas with that place*, Wiltshire Archaeological and Natural History Society, Local Committee

Farmer, D H, 1979, 'The refoundation of Amesbury Abbey', in Chandler, 1979b, 47-57

Field, J, 1972, *English field names: a dictionary*, David and Charles

Forde-Johnston, J, 1976, *Hill forts of the iron age in England and Wales: a survey of the surface evidence*, Liverpool University Press

Fowler, P J, 1971, 'Hill-forts AD 400-700', in Hill, D, and Jesson, M, (eds.) *The iron age and its hill-forts...*, Southampton University Archaeological Society, 203-13

Fuller, T, 1952, *The worthies of England*, Allen & Unwin

Gimpel, J, 1976, *The medieval machine: the industrial Revolution of the middle ages*, Gollancz

Godfrey, J, 1962, *The church in Anglo-Saxon England*, Cambridge University Press

Goodhugh, P S, 1970, 'The Poor Law in Amesbury', in *Wiltshire industrial archaeology*, no.2, 6-12

Goulstone, J, 1985, *The summer solstice games: a study of early English fertility religion*, author

Gover, J E B, *et al*, 1939, *The place-names of Wiltshire*, Cambridge University Press

Grinsell, L V, 1958, *The archaeology of Wessex*, Methuen

Hardy, T, 1906, *Jude the obscure*, Macmillan

Haslam, J, 1984, 'The towns of Wiltshire', in Haslam, J, (ed.) *Anglo-Saxon towns in southern England*, Phillimore, 87-147

Hinton, D A, 1977, *Alfred's kingdom: Wessex and the south, 800-1500*, Dent

Hinton, D A, 1979, 'Amesbury and the early history of its abbey', in Chandler, 1979b, 20-31

Hoare, Sir R C, 1826, *The history of modern Wiltshire: hundreds of Everley, Ambresbury and Underditch*, John Nichols

Hobsbawm, E J, and Rudé, G, 1973, *Captain Swing*, Penguin

Hogg, A H A, 1975, *Hill-forts of Britain*, Hart-Davis

Hoskins, W G, 1973, *Local history in England*, 2nd ed, Longman

Hughes, G W G, 1937, 'Notes on the courts leet and baron in Amesbury, Wilts', in *WAM*, vol.47, 521-5

Hunter-Mann, K, 1988, 'Excavation and fieldwork in Wiltshire, 1987: Amesbury: Vespasian's Camp', in *WAM*, vol.82, 176

Jackson, J E, 1867, 'Ambresbury monastery', in *WAM*, vol.10, 61-84

Jaggard, W R, 1921, *Experimental cottages: a report on the work of the department at Amesbury, Wiltshire*, HMSO (Department of Scientific and Industrial Research)

James, N D G, 1987, *Plain soldiering: a history of the armed forces on Salisbury Plain*, Hobnob Press

Jones, G, 1961, 'Settlement patterns in Anglo-Saxon England', in *Antiquity*, vol.35, 221-32

Kemm, W C, 1970, *Events relative to the town and inhabitants of Amesbury, Wilts, collated from slips written by William Cove Kemm of Amesbury (B.1813-D.1893)*, collated by Philip Dyke, typescript in WANHS Library

Kirby, J L, 1956, 'Clerical poll-taxes in the diocese of Salisbury, 1377-81', in Williams, N J, (ed.) *Collectanea*, WA&NHS Records Branch, (12), 157-67

Kite, E, 1899-1901, 'Notes on Amesbury monastery, with an account of some discoveries on the site in 1860', in *WNQ*, vol.3 *passim*

Kite, E, 1902-4, 'Amesbury monastery', in *WNQ*, vol.4, 74-80, 124-38

Knowles, D, 1963, *The monastic order in England*, 2nd ed, Cambridge University Press

Lewis, R A, 1957, 'County government since 1835', in *VCH Wilts*, vol.5, 231-92

Longmate, N, 1974, *The workhouse*, Maurice Temple Smith

Marsh, H, 1970, *Dark age Britain*, David and Charles

Mawer, A, and Stenton, F M, 1927, *The place-names of Worcestershire*, Cambridge University Press

Moon, A, 1977, 'Old railway lines', in Guthrie, J G S, (ed.) *What to see in and around Amesbury and Stonehenge*, Salisbury District Council, 28-31

Moore, N, 1976, 'Amesbury Abbey: an introduction to its buildings past and present', in *Hatcher Review*, no.1, 26-35

Morris, J, 1973, *The age of Arthur: history of the British Isles 350-650*, Weidenfeld and Nicolson

Myres, J N L, 1986, *The English settlements*, Clarendon Press

Noyes, E, 1913, *Salisbury Plain: its stones, cathedral city, villages and folk*, Dent

Oswald, A, 1975, *Clay pipes for the archaeologist*, British Archaeological Reports (14)

Parker, N, 1977, 'Military influence on Salisbury Plain', in Guthrie, J G S, (ed.) *What to see in and around Amesbury and Stonehenge*, Salisbury District Council, 24-7

Pevsner, N, 1975, *Wiltshire*, 2nd ed. revised by Bridget Cherry, Penguin

Pugh, R B, (ed.) 1947, *Calendar of Antrobus deeds before 1625*, WA&NHS Records Branch (3)

Pugh, R B, 1947-8, 'The early history of the manors in Amesbury', in *WAM*, vol.52, 70-110

Pugh, R B, 1956, 'The abbey, later priory, of Amesbury', *VCH Wilts*, vol.3, 242-59

Pugh, R B, (ed.) 1978, *Wiltshire gaol delivery and trailbaston trials, 1275-1306*, Wiltshire Record Society (33)

Ransome, M, (ed.) 1972, *Wiltshire returns to the bishop's visitation queries, 1783*, Wiltshire Record Society (27)

RCHM, 1979, Royal Commission on Historical Monuments (England), *Stonehenge and its environs*, Edinburgh University Press

RCHM, 1987, Royal Commission on the Historical Monuments of England, *Churches of south-east Wiltshire*, HMSO

Reeves, M E, 1956, 'Protestant nonconformity', in *VCH Wilts*, vol.3, 99-149

Richards, J, 1985, *Beyond Stonehenge*, Trust for Wessex Archaeology

Robinson, P H, 1984, 'Saxon coins of Edward the Elder from St Mary's churchyard, Amesbury', in *Numismatic chronicle*, 7th series, vol.144, 198-201

Rollason, D W, 1978, 'Lists of saints' resting places in Anglo-Saxon England', in *Anglo-Saxon England*, vol.7, 61-93

Ruddle, C S, 1893-5, 'Early tobacco pipes', in *WNQ*, vol.1, 281-2

Ruddle, C S, 1901, 'A census of Wilts in 1676', in *WNQ*, vol.3, 533-9

Scott, R, 1959, 'Medieval agriculture', in *VCH Wilts*, vol.4, 7-42

Short guide to the abbey church of St Mary and St Melor, [1978], Amesbury

Shute, H, 1986, *My lord Pembroke's manor of Netherhampton*, author

Soul, J, 1923, *Amesbury old and new: reminiscences and reflections*, Salisbury Times

Soul, J, 1926, *Amesbury historic and prehistoric*, Salisbury Times

Stafford, P A, 1978, 'The reign of Aethelred II, a study of the limitations on royal policy and action', in Hill, D, (ed.) *Ethelred the Unready: papers from the millenary conference*, British Archaeological Reports (59), 15-46

Stenton, F M, 1971, *Anglo-Saxon England*, 3rd ed, Oxford University Press

Stevens, E T, 1882, *Jottings on some objects of interest in the Stonehenge excursion*, Brown

Stone, J F S, 1958, *Wessex before the Celts*, Thames and Hudson

Talbot, C H, 1899-1904, 'Amesbury monastery', in *WNQ*, vol.3, 549-56; vol.4, 11-20

Thody, D W J, 1974, 'Railway reveries', in *Wiltshire industrial archaeology*, no.5, 35-42

Thorpe, P, 1979, *Moonraker firemen*, Wiltshire County Council

Turner, G L, 1911, *Original records of early nonconformity under persecution and indulgence*, Unwin

Wacher, J, 1978, *Roman Britain*, Dent

Webb, E D, 1890-3, 'Conventicles in Salisbury diocese (Wiltshire portion)', in *Transactions of the Salisbury Field Club*, vol.1, 36-44

Webb, S and B, 1929, *English poor law history*, 4 vols, Longman

Webster, G, and Dudley, D R, 1973, *The Roman conquest of Britain, AD 43-57*, revised ed, Pan

Wesley, J, 1909, *Journals*, vol.4, Dent

Whitlock, R, 1979, 'Just over the horizon: Amesbury, 1700-1979', in Chandler, 1979b, 70-81

Willoughby, R H W, 1971, 'Revd. Thomas Holland, a mechanical genius', in *WA&NHS bi-annual bulletin*, no.10, 10-11

Windley, E J, 1917, *Amesbury: its abbey, its church and its saint*, 3rd imp, Faith Press

Youings, J, 1972, *The dissolution of the monasteries*, Allen and Unwin

Index

NOTE: Place names are in Wiltshire unless otherwise stated; street, field and house names are in Amesbury unless otherwise stated. Maps and notes have not been indexed.

Abbey: Church: see Church; estate, 29; Lane, 122; Mansion (1660-1834), 25, 26, 31, 34, 45, 112-14; Mansion (from 1834) 1, 14, 15, 16, 26, 62, 72, 114; monastic house (979-1177), 8-12, 16, 17, 48, 103; monastic house (1177-1539): see Priory; park, 28, 31, 72, 111, 112; Square, 117, 118
Abraham, 103
Addison, Joseph, 46
Aelfthryth, 8, 9, 10, 103
Aeroplane and Armament Experimental Establishment, 79-80; see also Boscombe Down
Aethelred, 8
Aethelstan, 8
agriculture, 2, 3, 5, 10-11, 19-22, 29, 30-1, 33-4, 41, 48, 51, 75, 119-22
Agriculture and Fisheries, Ministry of, 81
Air Ministry, 80
Aldershot (Hants), 64
Alfred, 6
All-England Coursing Club, 125
Allington, 12, 67; Road, 148
Almanaze (Almond Hayes) Path, 114
Altcar (Lancs), 107
Amberley (Glos), 5
Ambri, Ambrius, 5, 17-18
Ambrosden (Oxon), 5
Ambrosiaci, 5
Ambrosius Aurelianus, 5-7, 17-18, 104
Amesbury: Board of Guardians, 42, 58, 125; Carnival Committee, 69; Earldoms (Earls) manor, 19, 23, 25, 52, 72, 118, 120; Electric Light Company, 63-5, 124, 125; Fife and Drum Band, 109; Fire Brigade, 44, 143, 146-7; Friendly Society, 118; Heaver, 31; Highway Board, 38; House, 137, 142, 152; hundred, 6, 10, 22; Motor Company, 130; name, 5; Parish Council, 64, 87, 108, 136; Priors (Priory) manor, 19, 24, 25, 36, 72, 87, 118, 120; Psalter, 97; Rural District Council, 147; Temperance Brass Band, 109; Town Brass Band, 109; Town Council, 65, 108; Town Silver Band, 109-10; Transport Company, 75, 83; Turnpike Trust, 26, 36-8, 71, 91, 125
Ancient Order of Foresters, 110
Andover (Hants), 8, 40, 42, 65
Andrews, Edwin, 28

Antrobus: Arms Hotel, 27, 28, 114, 115-17; deeds, 19, 22; (Sir) Edmund, 26-7, 29, 47, 65, 97, 114, 122; family, 26-7, 46, 97, 101, 114, 137; House, 27, 65; Road, 22, 27 apprenticing, 28, 29, 47
"Ark, The", 133
army, 40, 48, 79, 136
Arthur, 16, 104
Asher family, 27
Athelstan, 8
Aubrey, John, 35, 36
Augustine, 8
Avenue, The, 2, 54
Avon: Buildings, 147-8; River, 1, 2, 3, 7, 31, 33, 48, 52, 58, 72, 85, 87, 106, 107, 143; Temperance Hotel, 115; valley, 5, 6, 34, 48, 51, 75, 76
Avonstoke Close, 42, 58

Back Lane, 23, 33, 39, 47, 133, 136; see also School Lane
Bakehouse (Bakers) Lane, 33, 39, 43, 44, 67, 122, 137, 139, 148; see also Earls (Court) Road
Balet, John and Christine, 22
bands, 109-10
banking, 40, 130; see also names of banks
Barnard Field, 19, 30
barrows (tumuli), 2, 17, 52, 54, 85
Bartnett Field, 68
Basingstoke (Hants), 76, 79
Bath (Avon), 38; Road, 36
Batho, George Best, 28, 130
Battle of the Nile clumps, 54, 85
Bayley, Gabriel, 35
Beacon Hill, 6, 37, 48, 55, 75, 107
Bear Inn, 115
Beatrice, abbess, 12
Beauchamp, Bishop, 103
Becket, Thomas, 12, 16
Bedford, Duke of, 35, 36
Bedwyn, Great, 10, 11
Beggar's Opera, 26
Bell Hotel (Inn), 23, 151
bell-ringers, 102
Benedictine order, rule, 11, 12, 14
Berkshire, 12
"Birdcage Row", 149, 150
Birdlimes Farm, Porton, 45

160

Bishop, William, 144, 145
Black Cross Field, 19, 30, 69
Black Death, 24
Blake: farmer, 122; John, 29
Blatch, Mr, 121
blind house: *see* lock-up
Bloxham, Dr, 117
Blue Lion Inn, 58
Bocker Mead, 72
Boer War, 109
Bomber Command, 80
"Boneser", Joe, 148
Boney Mead, 111
Bonnewe, Florence, 24
borough, 22
Boscombe, 12; Down, 19, 48, 52, 79-80, 81; Down West, 79; Road, 31, 80
boundaries, 52-3
Bowcombe (Isle of Wight), 7
Bowles Hatches, 33
Boyle, Henry (Lord Carleton), 25, 72, 112
Bradenstoke, 18
Bremhill, 24
Bridgeman, Charles, 113
bridges, 7, 16, 26, 37, 71, 72, 86-7, 111, 112, 114
Bridgwater (Som), 37
Brigmerston, 2
Bristol (Avon), 5, 35, 76; Aeroplane Company, 143; Channel, 103
Brittany, 9, 17
Britton, John, 34
Broad Bridge, 87
Browne, Caroline, 46
Bruce family, 25
Buckland: Court, 65; Len, 132
Bugden's Motor Cycle Depot, 135
Bulford, 5, 12, 23, 37, 48, 69, 75, 76, 79, 85, 143; Camp, 48
bus station, 141, 143, 152
Butterfield, William, 90, 91, 93-5, 97-101
Butts, The, 106, 120
by-pass, 1, 70, 75, 85, 87, 133

Camden Town (London), 99
Cantilupe manor, 19
Cardynham (Cornwall), 103
Carleton, Lord (Henry Boyle), 25, 72, 112
carnivals, 108
Carpaccio, Cardinal, 103
Carpenter Street, 23
catholicism, 45, 85
Cemetery, 33, 111, 117; Corner, 86
Centre, The, 133-7
chapels: Primitive Methodist, 147; Wesleyan, 43, 45, 47, 125, 126; workhouse, 41, 60
charities, 46-7, 137

Charles, Prince, 110
children, 29-30, 41, 46-7, 60, 61
Childs, Asa, 121, 122, 129
Chilmark stone, 114
Chimes House, 63, 124, 125
Chippenham, 24
Chipperfield family, 143
Chisenbury Warren, 5
Chitterne, 36, 37
Cholderton, 70, 75
Chopping-Knife Inn, 41, 115
Choulston, 12
Church (Abbey Church, Parish Church), 1, 7, 10, 12, 15, 16, 18, 27, 33, 44-5, 46, 62, 90-105, 112; altar, 101; bosses, 103-4; chancel, 94-5, 96, 98, 100-1; chapels, 92, 94, 99, 100; clock, 95; corbels, 103-4; dedication, 90; fonts, 95-6, 100, 101; galleries, 97; glass, 101; Lane, 62, 114; links with abbey, 90; nave, 93-4, 96-9, 101, 103, 104; north aisle, 94, 96; north transept, 94, 99, 100; organ, 97, 99; piscinas, 96, 100, 101; pulpit, 98, 100; restorations, 90, 144; roofs, 90-1, 95, 97, 100, 101, 103, 104; Saxon work, 93, 101-3; screens, 98, 100, 101; south aisle, 93, 95-6, 97; south transept, 91-2, 95; Street, 33, 63, 106, 111-19; tower, 97, 101; wall-paintings, 97; yard, 37, 122
Chute Forest, 6
cinema, 63, 139-43, 147
Clack, 18
Clarence family, 19
Clarendon Forest, 6, 23
Clarke, William and Margaret, 23
clay pipes, 35-6, 129
"Cloisters" apartments, 85
coaches (stagecoaches), 36, 37-8
Cobbett, William, 34, 41
Cockle, Mrs, 47
Coldharbour, 22, 33, 43, 82-3, 137, 138, 143
Cole, Quint, 147
Colonial Restaurant, 75
Comilla House (New Inn), 36, 37, 72, 75, 130-2, 134
Coneybury, 2; Hill, 19
"Conygar" manor, 19
Cook, Thomas, 45
Cooper family, 27, 147
Co-operative Store (Kingsway House), 141, 144
Corfe Castle, 8
Corsham, 24
Coster, Henry, 99, 122
Countess: fair, 39, 106; (Court) Farm, 19, 27, 28, 29, 31, 69-71, 120; Field, 22, 30, 106; Road, 23, 31, 33, 37, 69-75, 79, 85, 87, 134, 135

161

coursing, 107, 125
Cox, William, 46
Coychurch (Mid-Glam), 103
Cread, Elizabeth, 28
cricket, 58, 106, 108, 109
Crooked Covert Copse, 136
Cuckold Hill, 120
Cursus, The, 2, 106

Dark Lane, 69, 120
Darrell, Joan, 24
Dawbeney: Mr, 52; Robert, 14, 16
Dawbeneys: manor, 19; mill, 86
Denham, Reg, 64
Despencer family, 19
Devizes, 35, 38, 61, 69
Diana House, 25, 72, 73
"Dick-a-Dick", 148
Domesday Book, 10-11, 62
Donhead, 24
Douglas: Archibald (Lord Douglas), 114; Charles, see Queensberry, 3rd Duke; William, see Queensberry, 4th Duke
Downton, 23
Drove, The, 75, 83
Druids: Lodge Camp, 48; Motel (Restaurant), 75, 85
Dunleys House, 115
Dunstan, 8
Durnford, 3, 11, 52, 58, 76, 85, 87; Path (Track), 57, 148
Durrington, 24, 76; Walls, 2, 5

Earldoms manor, see Amesbury
Earls (Court): Farm, 19, 22, 28, 29, 31, 43, 68, 120, 121; Road, 33, 39, 43, 67-8, 139; see also Bakehouse Lane
Earls Farm Down, 3, 5
East Kennett, 37
Edgar, 8, 9
Edmiston Road, 148
Edward: I, 14, 18; the Confessor, 10, 12; the Elder, 6; the Martyr, 8, 9
Edwards: Job, 15, 100, 139, 143; Road, 130, 139, 143
Eleanor of Provence, 14, 17
elections, 107
electricity supply, 63-5, 124, 127, 128, 136
Elfrida, see Aelfthryth Elizabeth I, 112
Elm Hays Field, 114
enclosure, 26, 30-1, 41, 52, 65, 68
Enford, 28
engine house, 43, 143
Ethelred, 8
Everleigh, 23
Exeter (Devon), 1, 37; Road, 31, 36
Eyers, William, 28
Eyres: family, 27; widow, 130

Fairholme, 46, 116
Fairlawn Hotel, 130
fairs, 22, 33, 38, 58, 67, 76, 106, 114, 125, 133, 137, 148
Field, Frank, 64
Fields: Betty, 143; Gracie, 143
fields, 19-22, 30, 33, 34, 52; see also individual field names
Figheldean, 2, 12
fire services, stations, 67, 139, 146-7
fires, 26, 27, 31, 38, 42-4, 45, 130, 133, 140, 143
fishing, 107
Fittleton, 37
Flitcroft: atlas, 19, 20-1, 30, 32-3; Henry, 113
Florak, Pontius, 18
Flower: Edward, 46, 47; Lane, 23, 33, 43, 87, 117, 130, 144-5, 147-8, 150, 152; see also Frog Lane, Tanner Lane
flower shows, 108, 109
Folly Bottom, 55, 75, 83
Fontevrault (France), 12, 13, 14; order of, 13-14, 16, 104
food, 42, 60
football, 106, 108, 109
Fovant House, 130
Fowle, (Rev) Fulwar W, 28, 45, 115
Fox, Edward, 35
Friar Tuck Cafe, 133
Frog Lane, 23, 33, 87, 117, 147; see also Flower Lane
Fuller, Thomas, 35

162

Gallows Hill, 85
Gane, Joseph, 28
gaol (lock-up), 38, 122, 123, 124, 125, 127, 137
garages, 129, 130, 133, 136, 149, 151, 152
Gauntlett: family, 35-6, 129; Hugh, 35, 36
Gay, John, 26, 113
Gay's Cave, 26
Geoffrey of Monmouth, 5, 17-18
George Hotel (Inn), 23, 28, 36, 38, 79, 125, 127, 128, 129
Giant's Dance, 17
Gilbert, Fanny, 29
Gilbertine order, 14
Glastonbury (Som), 17, 24
Gloucestershire, 95
Godric, 17
golf, 106
Grammar School, Old, 46, 130
Grateley (Hants), 48
Great: Bedwyn, 10, 11; Boney Meadow, 121; Durnford, see Durnford; Western Railway, 76
Green, Charles, 99
Grey Bridge, 16, 71, 72, 114
Greyhound Inn, 137, 138
Guinevere, 7, 16, 17, 18, 101

Half Borough Field, 19, 30
Ham Hatches, 33, 85, 86, 87
Haradon Hill, 6, 75
Hardy, Thomas, 38
Harnham, 80
Harrison: John, 122; Richard, 47
Harrow Way, 2, 3
hatches, 33
Hayes family, 114
Hays, Mr, 117
Hayward, Mr, 120
health centre, 137
Hell (field name), 33
Henry: II, 12, 13; VIII, 24
Hertford: Earl of, 25, 72, 112; Marquess of, 112
Heytesbury, 23, 37
Hibberd, Ted, 64
Hicks, - 132
High Street, 1, 7, 23, 33, 36, 43, 45, 46, 63, 118, 122-33, 134, 143
Highfield Road, 68, 69
Hillary, Joseph, 29
hillforts, 3, 5, 19
Hindon, 23
Holders Road, 39, 79, 81-2, 83, 108
Holland, (Rev) Thomas, 43, 44-5, 100, 147
Home Farm Model Dairies, 79
Hopper, Thomas, 114
Hough, William, 130

housing, 51-2, 69, 80, 81-2; experimental, 81; ribbon, 69, 83; see also urban development; and individual road names
hundred, 6, 10, 22
Hutchins, Mr, 121

Idmiston, 67
inns, 23, 25, 29, 39; see also individual inns
insurance, 44
Ireland, 17, 103
Irish Sea, 103
Isabel of Lancaster, 14
Italy, 103
Ivydene Hotel, 43, 44, 140, 143-4, 147

Jennings and Kent, 133
Jockey Inn, 46, 130
Jones, Inigo, 112
Judas Iscariot, 104

Kemm, William Cove, 15-16, 36, 39, 125, 129
Kemm's Square, 152
Kennet and Amesbury Trust, 37
Kent House, 25, 72, 74, 114, 123: Farm (Park Farm), 31, 72, 74
Kenton, Anthony Cook, 130
Kent's Chamber, 101
Kilford family, 27
Kings Arms Inn, 117, 122
King's Island, 52, 120; Hatches, 33
Kingsway House (Co-operative Store), 144
Kintbury (Berks), 12
Kitchener Road, 75, 83, 136
Knook, 5

Lacock, 18
Lake, 57; Down Camp, 48
Lancaster: family, 19; Joseph, 46
Lancelot, 17
Land Settlement Act, 81
Larkhill, 37, 48, 79, 143
laundry, 62, 136
legends, 7, 9, 16-18
Lesser Cursus, 2
library, 137, 139
Lime Kiln Hill, 57
Little: Field, 120; Thatch, 111
Lloyds Bank, 117, 118, 151
lock-up (blind house, gaol), 38, 122, 123, 124, 125, 127, 137
Logans DIY Store, 143, 152
London, 1, 35, 76; and South Western Railway, 48, 76; Road, 6, 31, 33, 37, 52, 62, 72, 75, 79, 81, 83-5, 134; Way, 75
Long: Ann, 28; Thomas, 45; William, 31
Longspee, William (Earl of Salisbury), 22
Lord's Walk, 25, 72, 85, 135

163

Louvain (Belgium), 26, 45
Lower: Camp Site, 80; Fold, 72
Lynchets, 58, 67, 122; Road, 69
Lynchfield Road, 69
Lyndhurst (Hants), 7
Lyneham, 18

Maddington, 12
Maggs, James, 29
Malmesbury, 12, 24
Malory, Thomas, 17
manorial courts, 22, 69, 118, 119-22, 137, 148
manors, 19, 25; *see also* individual manors
market, 22, 34, 38-40, 67, 76, 83, 87, 106, 125, 148, 152; house, 33, 38, 118, 119, 121, 148; place, 22, 27, 33, 38, 118, 122, 137, 148-9
Marlborough, 23, 24, 36; Downs, 2; Street, 23, 125
Martlesham Heath (Suffolk), 80
Mary, daughter of Edward I, 14, 18
Matravers, Agnes, 132
Melksham, 24
Melor, St, 7, 9, 15, 16-18, 22, 38, 90, 97, 103
Merchant: family, 144; Mr, 47
Merchants Cottage, 144
Mere, 23, 24, 37
Merlin, 7, 17, 18
Meyrick, Arthur, 46, 116-17
Midland Bank, 125, 127
Mid-Southern Utilities Ltd, 64
milestones, 37, 85
Mill Lane, 147
Millards Cafe, 75
millennium celebrations, 110
mills, 11, 19, 28, 33, 40, 57-8, 62-3, 86, 112; *see also* individual mills
Milston, 2, 46
minster, 7, 10, 12, 103
Moffatt, W B, 60
Monica, Sister, 45
Monk, Alfred, 99
Montagu family, 19
Montague, Sybil, 14
Moor Hatches, 34
Morris, (Dr) Claver, 125
Morte d'Arthur, 17
mortuary, 58, 60
Mullens Pond (Hants), 36
Mundy family, 27
museum, 65

NAAFI complex, 83
Neighbour, (Dr) Philip, 75
Netheravon, 11, 44, 79
Nevill family, 19
New: Covert, 5; Forest Coursing Club, 125; Inn (Comilla House, *qv*), 36, 37, 75, 122, 131, 132; Inn (present), 125; Leaze, 120; Theatre Ballroom, 130
Newton Toney, 48, 67, 79; Road, 148
Nile clumps, Battle of the, 54, 85
Normandy, 13
Normanton, 36, 52, 85; Field, 30
Northams Close, 31, 122
Northumbria, 103
Noyes, Ella, 38

Ogbury Camp, 3
Old: Grammar School, 46, 130; Marlborough Road, 23, 57, 67, 69; Sarum, 3, 6, 10, 18, 37, 65
"Old Q", 26
"Olde Shoppe, The" (bakery), 144, 152
Olding: Edmund, 28, 31; Joseph, 28
Osgood: J, 70; John, 121
Osmund, St, 11
Oxford, 95

Packway, 75
Pancet, 23
Paradice Mead, 33
Parish Church, *see* Church
Park: see Abbey; Farm, *see* Kent House
Parsonage: Barn, 68; Close, 68; house, *see* vicarage; Lane (Road), 68-9, 120
Parsons, George, 114
Penchet, 23
Pertuht, Thomas, 22
Pewsey, 48, 76; Vale, 5
Philpot, - 152
Phoenix Cottage, 115, 116
Pickfords depository, 67
Pike: family, 27; George, 29; William, 28
pilgrims, 16-17
Pinckney: family, 116; Mr, 122; Robert, 28, 31
Pink House, 89, 111
pipes, clay, 35-6, 129
Plaza cinema, 63, 139-43, 147
police, 29, 65, 122, 136-7
Poore, Mr, 122
poorhouse, 41
population, 1, 3, 11, 23-4, 27-30, 31, 33, 44, 45
Porton, 45, 67; Down, 52; Farm, 121
Portsmouth (Hants), 62
post office, postal service, 40, 43, 44, 47, 117, 130, 131, 144
Pouncette Street, 18, 23
pound, 121, 122, 144
poverty, 28, 30, 31, 41-2, 60-1; *see also* workhouse
prehistory, 1-3, 52-4
Preseli Mountains (Dyfed), 2
Priors manor, *see* Amesbury

164

Priory (1177-1539), 13-17, 18, 23, 24, 25, 33, 44, 48, 87, 117, 122, 125, 132, 148; dissolution, 24, 25; position, 14-16, 104-5, 114; *see also* Abbey, Church
Public Assistance Institution, 42; *see also* workhouse
Purdue, Charles, 29
Purnell, Joseph, 28
Pyle, (Dr) Charles, 28, 130

Queens Falls, 112
Queensberry: Bridge, 7, 26, 37, 111, 112; 3rd Duchess (Catherine), 26, 113; 3rd Duke (Charles Douglas), 26, 31, 37, 113-14, 122; 4th Duke (William Douglas), 26, 37, 41, 114; Hotel, 152

railway, 38, 48, 75-9; narrow gauge, 62-3, 111; station, 75, 77-9
Ramsbury, 103
Randall, Edward, 147
Ratfyn, 2, 45, 52, 64, 69, 79; Down, 52; Farm, 22, 27, 28, 29, 31, 76, 121; Road, 23, 82, 85
Rattue family, 27
Rawlings, Mary, 28
recreation, 58, 106-9; ground, 33, 85-6, 108-9, 111
Red House Farm, 28, 29, 31, 58, 65, 66, 79, 121; Aerodrome, 79
Rede, John, 45
Redworth House, 147
religion, 44-5; *see also* chapels; Church
riots, agricultural, 31, 34, 41
river, see Avon
roads, 2, 11, 23, 36-8, 48, 51, 52, 55, 69, 122; *see also* individual roads
Robin Hood's Ball, 2
Robinson's (chemists), 130
Rolfe: Arthur, 64; family, 27
Rollestone Camp, 48, 79
Romano-British period, 3, 5, 6, 55
Romsey (Hants), 9
Rooke, Michael, 28
rope-walk, 149
Rose, John, 46
Rose's Grammar School, 46, 130
royal premises, 7, 10
Ruddle, (Rev) C S, 101
Rushall, 37, 38
Rushworth, Patience, 28

"St Michael of Amesbury", 132
Salisbury, 1, 19, 23, 24, 35, 37, 38, 40, 44, 48, 57, 69, 76, 79, 80, 99, 143, 144, 147; and South Wiltshire Museum, 75; District Council, 147; Earls of, 19, 22; Plain, 1, 5, 36, 48, 55, 57, 75, 76, 79, 130; Road, 33, 58, 61, 63, 65-7, 68, 139, 152; Street, 22, 23, 33, 38, 43, 63, 118, 123, 130, 133, 136, 137, 139, 148-52; Way, 121
Sandell: family, 125; Joseph, 28; Mary, 111; Misses, 46
Saracen's Head Inn, 117
Saucer, Robert, 23
Saxon: cemetery, 6; coins, 6; crosses, 6, 101-3; period, 6-10
Scanes, farmer, 120-1
School Lane, 23, 33, 39, 47, 64, 65, 130, 133, 136-7; *see also* Back Lane
schools, 28, 29, 30, 41, 46-7, 60, 61, 68, 83, 89, 90, 97, 111, 116-17, 130, 133, 136-7, 149, 152
Scientific and Industrial Research, Department of, 81
Scott, (Sir) George Gilbert, 60
Selfe, Henry, 28, 31
Selwood, see Zilwood
Seymour: Edward, 25, 112; John, 25; (Sir) William, 25, 112
Shaftesbury (Dorset), 9, 24, 45
Shallow Water Meadow, 122
shops, 39-40; *see also* trades and trading; and descriptions under relevant street
Shrewton, 2, 37, 48, 75, 76
Simmance, Harold, 39
Sloans Garage, 130
Smeaton, John, 111
Smith: Doug, 64; Robert, 35
Smithfield Street, 23, 33, 43, 137-44
Smokey Joe's, 75
Snook, George, 64
social structure, 11, 19, 27-30
Solstice Farm estate, 80
Somerset, 95; Dukes of, 25; Protector, 25
Soper, Walton, 129
Soul, John, 117
South Ham: Farm, 31; Field, 19, 30; Street, 23
South Mill, 27, 28, 33, 57-8, 62-5, 87; cottage, 58; Green, 58; Hill, 3, 27, 41, 52, 53, 57-9, 122; Hill Field, 22, 122; Lane (Road), 33, 58, 62, 65, 148; Woods, 53
Southampton (Hants), 38
Southams Close, 31
Southern Electricity Board, 65
Souths manor, 19
Sparey, Ernest, 64
sports, 106-8; centre, 108-9
Spratt, Henry, 46
Spreadbury (Spredbury): family, 27; Joseph, 114
stagecoaches, 36, 37-8
Stallard, William, 132
station, *see* bus, fire, railway
Stockport Bottom, 67

165

stocks, 119, 122
Stonehenge, 2, 5, 16, 17, 18, 31, 37, 39, 48, 54, 55, 65, 106, 109, 125; Camp, 48, 79; Road, 3, 37, 62, 85-7, 89, 111, 148; Temperance Hotel, 126
streetlighting, 64
streets (in general), 22-3; *see also* roads; and individual streets
Stukeley, William, 34
Swan Inn, 23, 35, 36, 152
Swindon, Marlborough and Everleigh Trust, 37

Tanner, Thomas, 28, 31
Tanners Lane, 43, 87, 122, 144, 147; *see also* Flower Lane
tanyards, 125, 148
taxation, 24
telephone exchange, 147
temperance hotels, 40, 43, 115, 126
tennis, 108
Three: Cups Inn, 23; Tuns Inn, 125
Thruxton (Hants), 37
Tilshead, 10, 11
tithe barn, 91
tobacco, 35
tollgates, 29, 38, 69
tollhouses, 37, 58, 65, 69, 71, 89, 111, 148
Totterdown, 2
town, growth of, *see* urban development
Townsend (Town End): Field, 120; Little Field, 22, 136; Mill, 57, 62 trades and trading, 11, 22, 27, 28-9, 38-40, 76, 148; *see also* market, shops; and individual traders
Trowbridge, John, 31
Truckle: family, 27; Moses, 29
Tucker, Frank, 134, 135, 136
tumuli (barrows), 2, 17, 52, 54, 85
Turner, Mary, 28
turnpikes, 26, 36-8, 58, 65, 69, 85, 86, 111, 122; see also tollgates, tollhouses

Ugford, 18
Underwood, G W, 130, 133
Upavon, 2, 79
Upper Fold, 72
urban development, 7, 10, 18-19, 22-4, 28, 32-3, 51-2, 153

Vespasian, 3
Vespasian's Camp, 3, 5-7, 19, 85, 87, 113
vicarage (parsonage house): former, 16, 28, 45, 91, 114-15; present, 114
Victoria, Queen, 27
Vincent, widow, 125
Vine Cottage, 147
Viney: Ann, 30; family, 67
Vineys (Vinons) Farm, 23, 28, 66, 67

Wales, 2
Walker, J, 99
Waltham (Essex), 12
Wanborough, 24
War: Department (Office), 48, 76; memorial, 140, 142
Warne, William, 120
Washington, (Sir) Lawrence, 52
watermeadows, 21, 33-4, 111
Webb, John, 26, 112, 114
weighbridge, weighing engine, 38, 119, 148
Wesley, John, 45
Wessex: culture, 2; Electricity Company, 64-5
West Amesbury, 19, 24, 36, 45, 52, 54, 57, 76, 85, 87-8, 148; Farm, 27, 28, 29, 31; fields, 19; House, 87-8
West Mill, 33
Westbury, 48, 76
Weymouth (Dorset), 99
Wherwell (Hants), 8, 103
White Hart Inn, 130
Whitnam, *see* Wittenham
William: I, 10; of Malmesbury, 17
Willoughby Hedge, 37
Wilsford, 57
Wilton, 9, 10, 12, 18, 24, 65; House, 45
Wilts and Dorset Bank, 130
Wiltshire: County Council, 42, 47, 133, 147; William, 132
Winchester (Hants), 9
Windsor, Dean and Canons of, 44
Winterbourne: Bassett, 12; Gunner, 57
Winterslow, 12
Witham Friary (Som), 12
Wittenham: Bank, 122; Path, 62, 87, 89, 111, 148
Woodford, 2, 57, 58, 76
Woodhenge, 2, 52, 54
Woods, "Bungy", 62-3, 83-5, 111
Wood-way, 87, 148
workhouse, 27, 28, 29, 30, 31, 41-2, 46, 48, 58-61, 63
Wrestler's Gate, 36
Wylye, 37
Wyndersham House, 46

Yarham: Misses, 125; Sally, 126
Yew Cottage, 68
YMCA buildings, 85, 135

Zilwood (Selwood): F, 16; family, 46, 152; John, 15, 46

166